Listening to Others

Listening to Others

Developmental and Clinical Aspects of Empathy and Attunement

Edited by

Salman Akhtar

Jason Aronson

Lanham • Boulder • New York • Toronto • Plymouth, UK

Published in the United States of America
by Jason Aronson
An imprint of Rowman & Littlefield Publishers, Inc.

A wholly owned subsidiary of
The Rowman & Littlefield Publishing Group, Inc.
4501 Forbes Boulevard, Suite 200, Lanham, Maryland 20706
www.rowmanlittlefield.com

Estover Road
Plymouth PL6 7PY
United Kingdom

British Library Cataloguing in Publication Information Available

Library of Congress Cataloging-in-Publication Data

Listening to others : developmental and clinical aspects of empathy and attunement / edited by Salman Akhtar.
p. ; cm.
Includes bibliographical references and index.
ISBN-13: 978-0-7657-0514-3 (cloth : alk. paper)
ISBN-10: 0-7657-0514-1 (cloth : alk. paper)
ISBN-13: 978-0-7657-0515-0 (pbk. : alk. paper)
ISBN-10: 0-7657-0515-X (pbk. : alk. paper)
1. Psychotherapist and patient. 2. Psychoanalysis. 3. Listening. 4. Empathy. I. Akhtar, Salman, 1946 July 31-
[DNLM: 1. Communication. 2. Psychoanalytic Therapy—methods. 3. Empathy. 4. Professional-Patient Relations. 5. Psychoanalytic Theory. WM 460.5.C5 L773 2006]
RC480.8.L56 2007
616.89'14—dc22 2006035244

Printed in the United States of America

™ The paper used in this publication meets the minimum requirements of American National Standard for Information Sciences—Permanence of Paper for Printed Library Materials, ANSI/NISO Z39.48-1992.

To

the memory of

Margaret S. Mahler and Selma Kramer

Contents

Acknowledgments

The chapters in this book were originally presented at the Thirty-seventh Annual Margaret S. Mahler Symposium on Child Development held on April 8, 2006, in Philadelphia. First and foremost, therefore, we wish to express our gratitude to the Margaret S. Mahler Psychiatric Research Foundation. We are also grateful to Michael Vergare, M.D., Chairman, Department of Psychiatry and Human Behavior, Jefferson Medical College, as well as to the Psychoanalytic Center of Philadelphia for their shared sponsorship of the symposium. Many colleagues from the Psychoanalytic Center of Philadelphia helped during the symposium, and we remain grateful to them. Finally, we wish to acknowledge our sincere appreciation to Melissa Nevin for her efficient organization and assistance during the symposium and for her outstanding skills in the preparation of this book's manuscript.

I

THE 'LISTENING CURE'

An Overview

Salman Akhtar, M.D.

Freud's celebrated patient, Anna O., designated psychoanalysis to be a "talking cure" (Breuer and Freud, 1893–1895). She was right insofar as psychoanalysis does place verbal exchange at the center stage. Indeed the "fundamental rule" (Freud, 1913, p. 134) of analytic technique is that the patient must free-associate and must not censor what comes to mind. He or she must not deliberately avoid talking about something on syntactical, aesthetic, and moral grounds. Freud's stern injunction to the patient was: "never forget that you have promised to be absolutely honest, and never leave anything out because, for some reason or another, it is unpleasant to tell it" (1913, p. 135). The counterpart to such verbal offerings of the patient were the analyst's spoken words. Such 'interventions' were varied and, with the maturation of psychoanalysis as a clinical discipline, a great variety of them gradually evolved. Bibring's (1953) categorization of analytic interventions into five types (namely, abreaction, suggestion, manipulation, clarification, and interpretation) constituted just the beginning of this list. The concept of 'interpretation' alone was broken down into the subcategories of anagogic interpretation, transference interpretation, extra-transference interpretation, deep interpretation, genetic interpretation, and so on. As if this was not enough, further types of interventions got evolved including construction, reconstruction, bridging intervention, affirmative intervention, depth-rendering intervention, developmental intervention, and the like.

While this plethora of terminology validated Anna O.'s astute observation, it also did a bit of harm. By focusing upon the patient's and therapist's *speaking* activities, this emphasis diverted attention from how the two parties *listen* to each other. The following questions thus got ignored: Is analytic listening different from ordinary listening? What are the prerequisites for analytic listening? Is only one type of listening required during analytic sessions? If there are more than one type of listening required, then what determines the use of one particular type at a given moment? What is one listening for? Does one listen to words, gaps between words, or the music of affect that pervades the analytic session? Can one 'listen' to silences, visual images, postural changes, and other nonverbal communications? Should one's listening attitude change during an extra-analytic encounter with the patient? How does one or the other variety of listening affect one's interventions? And, so on and so forth.

One can add some patient-focused questions on the topic as well. Does the patient actually listen when the analyst speaks? Always? Does the patient listen to the analyst's words or his or her tone of voice? How does the patient listen to himself or herself? Are the patients' listening skills characterological in origin, or can they be enhanced by analysis itself? To be sure, this list can be readily expanded.

The point is that while what Anna O. said was true, it hardly constitutes the 'whole truth' to use a forensic expression. Psychoanalysis is a listening *and* talking cure. Freud knew this and, unlike his patient, emphasized both elements as integral to clinical work. In a characteristically pithy remark, he stated that the analyst "must adjust himself to the patient as a telephone receiver is adjusted to the transmitting microphone" (1912, pp. 115–116). Listening with no talking can only go this far. Talking without listening can mislead and harm.

One thing is clear. A maternal sort of holding of the psychically banished elements has to precede a meaningful examination of them with the aim of deeper self-understanding. Credulous listening must precede skeptical listening. Consolidation must come before deconstruction, empathy before insight, affirmation before interpretation and "containing-holding before transformative looking" (Wright, 1991, p. 300). In working with patients with well-established object constancy, the oscillations between these two poles of attention and intervention are mild; to extend a developmental metaphor, the 'mother' is already present with the child in the room and 'father' can proceed with his entertaining and educative distractions. In sicker patients, however, maternal "homeostatic attunement" has to be established before the introduction of paternal "disruptive attunement" (Herzog, 1984). In either case, psychoanalytic treatment always requires both types of listening (credulous and skeptical) and intervening (affirmative and interpretive). A psychoanalytic technique that opts for only one side of this duality misses the clinical boat, even if it rests safely on the shores of a pristine theory.

BETWEEN HEARING AND UNDERSTANDING

In an attempt to find preliminary answers to some of the questions raised here, let us begin with a statement that is so self-evident as to border on being comical. The first requirement for listening is an intact capacity for hearing. While lapses of hearing owing to extraneous noise are excusable, those caused by 'internal noise' constitute contertransference resistance and need self-analytic attention, supervision, and consultation with colleagues. The possibility of an actual hearing impairment must also be considered in this context. Not infrequently one comes across analysts with hearing aids though one can never be confident about the efficiency of these devices in the clinical situation. More distressing is the encounter with analysts who do not wear hearing aids but seem to be suffering from mild to moderate hearing loss. This is often politely tolerated by their analytic peers to a much greater extent than a surgical practice group's tolerance would be of a colleague's hand tremors. Some further attention toward this matter is clearly needed on the part of various ethics and 'impaired analyst' committees of the analytic societies.

Moving on to psychological matters, one has to raise the question whether analytic listening is different from ordinary listening. To this, my answer is 'yes' and 'no.' I say 'yes' because listening during psychoanalysis has

- an entirely different sort of verbal material (i.e., that produced as a result of free association) as its subject,
- both conscious and unconscious aspects of what is being communicated under its purview,
- a purpose that is different from that of ordinary listening,
- implicit and explicit consent from the one who is talking that one can listen to him in more than a superficial way, and
- a receptive organ in the form of the analyst's mind which is not only giving an "evenly suspended attention" (Freud, 1912, p. 111) to the patient's material but is itself mellowed by a certain amount of "regression in the service of the other" (Olinick, 1969).

Since none of these conditions apply to listening in ordinary circumstances (e.g., when one is listening to a neighbor, a grocery store clerk, an accountant), analytic listening appears to be a very different kind of receptive activity. Ordinary listening is sharply focused, consciousness-oriented, avoidant of 'deeper' meanings, and essentially transactional even if guided by empathy and civil constraints. Psychoanalytic listening is quite the opposite.

Having said this, I hasten to add that analytic listening is also *not* different from 'ordinary listening'; the latter actually constitutes an important aspect of the analytic listening. In other words, sometimes the analyst becomes quite focused and almost attends exclusively to the surface material. At other times, his attention is toward deeper and hidden messages. Seen this way, psychoanalytic listening, like psychoanalytic intervening, appears to be a fluid combination of spontaneity and deliberateness, with variable attention toward conscious and unconscious communications. It is in this context that differences in analytic style make their appearance. Klauber (1968) has captured the essence of this issue in the following succinct passage.

> The degree to which analysis of conscious and preconscious attitudes should be allowed to shade off into discussion of the patient's problems depends upon the theoretical orientation of the psychoanalyst. For those analysts for whom interpretation is orientated to the ego, it seems inevitable for the accurate clarification of the unconscious should be fully explored. Other psychoanalysts might dispute the appropriateness of the discussion of the patient's problems of which some analysts approve and consider it a degradation of psychoanalytic technique. (p. 137)

Underlying such variations of technique are different attitudes toward the patient's verbalizations and different styles of listening. One attitude prompts skepticism and a listening geared to decipher "the ways in which the patient's wishes and fantasies colour his perception of reality, past or present" (Strenger, 1989, p. 603). The other attitude mobilizes credulousness and a listening geared to discern "the healthy striving for wholeness and psychic survival" (Strenger, 1989, p. 603) in the patient's communications. The recent Arlow-Schwaber debate (Arlow, 1995; Schwaber, 1998) exemplifies this very polarity in the analyst's listening attitude. With a different slant, Spencer and Balter (1990) also underscore the tension between the "introspective" and the "behavioral" methods of observation in psychoanalysis. In the former, the analyst puts him or herself in the position of the analysand and derives clinical understanding from the latter's perspective. In the latter, the analyst adopts the "view of a spectator, without regard to the subject's own thoughts or feelings" (p. 402). The two methods, often yielding different sets of information, are complementary, each modifying the other in the service of deepening the grasp of the analysand's mental functioning.

VARIABLES THAT CAN ALTER LISTENING

Putting aside the extraneous factor of actual noise within (e.g., a brash air conditioner) or outside (e.g., building construction, major road repairs) the office and the organic factor of impaired hearing, one can discern at least four psychosocial variables that can significantly alter the listening capacity and attitude of the analyst.

Characterological resistance

Listening is fundamentally a maternal activity. It requires putting one's own concerns aside and cultivating at a sense of devotion to the other; Winnicott's (1960) phrase the "ordinary devoted mother" readily comes to mind in this context. Listening requires opening one's heart and mind to someone else and taking in their mental content; the metaphor of a receptive maternal vagina that grasps father's penis is also hard to overlook here. Listening requires not being in a hurry to interrupt the narrative, to question, to arrive at conclusions, and to give the material being offered a readily well-polished form. All these qualities, namely, devotion, receptivity, and containing without rushing to 'explain,' are characteristically maternal, hence feminine. Well-developed capacity for listening therefore requires characterological comfort with feminine identifications, regardless of one's actual gender.

A related facet of listening is the 'ingestion' of someone else's spoken words. Such openness also has the remote echoes of an infant gladly taking in the maternal breast. Good capacity for listening therefore also emanates from comfort with one's orally receptive infantile self-representations. Yet another element in listening is a certain amount of slowing down, an unhurried sort of mentation, or to borrow a phrase from Mahler et al. (1975), a certain "low keydness." Absence of internal noise (and tolerance of what noise does exist within oneself) therefore enhance the capacity of listening.

In essence, good capacity for listening comes from a character organization that has peacefully assimilated early identifications with a devoted mother, accepted at an archaic but deep level the imago of a receptive maternal vagina, is unafraid of one's own baby-on-the-breast self-representation, and does not rely upon "manic defense" (Klein,

1935; Winnicott, 1935) on a habitual basis. Too conflicted (or deficient) maternal identifications, too anxiety-producing infantile self-representations, too intense a denial of maternal sexuality, and too much use of manic defense lead to a characterological style that is unsuited for the act of listening.

Conceptual rigidity

Strict allegiance to one or the other psychoanalytic model can also impair listening. Look at the following examples. An 'ego psychologist' sees only drive-defense sort of compromises in the patient's material. A 'Kernbergian' sees idealization as a defense against regression and a 'Kohutian' sees it as a resumption of a thwarted developmental need. A 'Mahlerian' regards patients' fluctuating levels of intimacy as representing merger-abandonment anxieties while a 'relationist' sees a craftily enacted scenario of mutual teasing and seduction in the same oscillation. A 'Kleinian' views patients' hatred of the analyst's silence as an envious attack on a withholding breast while a 'Winnicottian' views that very outrage as manifestation of hope (that the analyst can 'survive' the patient's assault) and therefore of love!

Admittedly, these are caricatures. Nonetheless the point I am trying to make is a serious one: a rigid allegiance to one or the other type of analytic thinking can narrow the way one listens to the patient. Worse, it can lead to a situation where the analyst does not listen at all because his theory offers him a prepackaged and formulaic understanding. To put it bluntly: Any analyst who really listens to his or her patient cannot be rigidly committed to any theoretical model. Genuine respect for all such models without exclusive commitment to any of them is the only assurance that one can truly listen to what the patient is trying to convey. Pine's (1988) cogent reminder that psychoanalysis has "four psychologies" (drive, ego, object relations, and the self) and that each of these demand listening and speaking rights in the clinical arena must be kept in mind.

Countertransference blocks

Freud's (1910, p. 145) grim warning that "no psychoanalyst goes further than his own complexes and resistances permit" highlights how personal problems on the other side of the couch can impede proper listening and intervening. Racker (1968) went on to distinguish two types of countertransference blocks to the receptivity of the analyst. Concordant "countertransference" responses are those in which the analyst identifies with the patient's own central feeling state. "Complimentary" countertransferences result from the analyst's identification with a significant object that is projected into him by the patient. In the former, the analyst identifies with the patient's self-representation and in the latter with the patient's object representation. While partial and transient identifications of this sort can help develop empathy for the patient's inner experience, unquestioned and total identifications in this regard make listening peacefully to the patient difficult. The reason for mentioning these well-established observations is to balance the current enthusiasm about the informative potential of countertransference since that seems to have eclipsed the fact that countertransference can also impede listening.

Cultural differences

Listening can also be affected by cultural difference within the clinical dyad. This is most clearly evident in the treatment of bilingual patients (Amati-Mehler et al., 1993). Denotations, connotations, aphorisms, colloquialisms, proverbs, curse words, and terms of endearment as well as the mere prosodic qualities of language, all enter into how one speaks and how ones' spoken words are received and processed by the listener. While the impact of the patient's bilingualism has received attention, it is only recently that the analyst's bilingualism and its impact on his listening and intervening activities has been brought forth for consideration (Akhtar, 2006).

Linguistic difference, however, is not the only 'cultural' variable that can alter the analyst's listening. Matters of nationality, social class, race, ethnicity, aesthetic preferences, and politics can also have an impact upon the empathy and attunement of the analyst (Abbasi, 2007; Akhtar, 1999; Gorkin, 1996; Roland, 1996). Subtle, or not too subtle, prejudices on the analyst's part can get mobilized when differences along these dimensions exist and preclude a stance of neutrality vis-à-vis the patient's material.

Far from being matters of expressive idiom and unobjectionable aspects of lifestyle, the value system of the dyad affects the clinical exchange in significant, if subtle, ways. Patient's value system and

> ideals may take forms compatible or incompatible with the ideals of individual analysts: propensities toward austerity or luxury, toward the acceptance or non-acceptance of commonly held standards of choice of work, or even of dress, which may be treated by one psychoanalyst as symptoms and by another with toleration. (Klauber, 1968, p. 131)

Values of the sort that can affect listening are the product of the socioeconomic status, parental dictates and lifestyles, era and nation in which one has been raised and is practicing, educational institutions attended, and superego modification via extra-familial identifications during late adolescence and early adulthood. However, religion also plays a role here. If, for instance, the analyst is indifferent or hostile to religion, he is likely to be highly skeptical toward his analysand's spiritual yearnings. He may side step such issues, subtly devalue them, or quickly reduce them to their alleged instinctual origins. On the other hand, if the analyst is religious, his attitude toward such associations is likely to be more tolerate and permissive. Matters involving abortion, homosexuality, impending death, and life after death, especially tend to evoke countertransference reactions that are, at least in part governed by the analyst's religious beliefs. The specific religion to which the analyst belongs can also come to play an important, even if subtle, role in his listening to patient's views on political conflicts involving their two religious groups (Akhtar, 2007).

AN UNEXPLORED POSSIBILITY

Having elucidated the developmental underpinnings of the capacity to listen, the types of listening, and the factors that can impede effort to listen, I move on to a provocative but serious and hitherto unexplored technical possibility. This pertains to the analyst's letting the patient know that he (or she) refuses to listen to the patient's material. The mere mention of such an intervention is sure to horrify most, if not all, psychoanalysts. Therefore let me quickly explain what I mean by this innovation, under what circumstances it might be indicated, and what is the theoretical rationale and technical yield of it.

The conditions under which the analyst, I believe, might openly declare that he refuses to listen include the following: (i) when the patient is repeating himself or herself ad nauseam (just recall patients who explain all the reasons why they feel unloved by their spouses over and over and over again!), (ii) when the patient is deriving sexually perverse gratification from the act of speaking itself, and (iii) when the patient is expressing a transference-based distortion after it has been analyzed (and the underlying meanings mutually agreed upon) a hundred times or more. The last mentioned point cannot be overemphasized. The 'refusal to listen' is a technical strategy reserved for later phases of long analyses; years of patient listening, affirmative interventions, and interpretive work must precede the use of this last ditch maneuver. Even under these circumstances, the analyst does not actually stop listening. What he does stop is listening to the surface material. The analyst, who has heard five hundred times about a parent's indifference toward the patient, might raise his hand and say "You know what, I am really not interested in listening to this tale all over again but I am very interested in why you feel driven to tell it to me again and again as if I have never heard it."

The theoretical rationale for doing so consists of the fact that listening, like all other human functions, can become delinked from ego control and come to lie under the domination of id or superego. In other words, the function of listening can become instinctualized. One might go on listening to such complaints (forever!) as a form of masochistic submission to the patient. One might also keep on listening eternally to repetitions and verbal enactments of the sort mentioned above because one has come to idealize listening; the more one listens the better one is in the eyes of internalized analytic ideals. This complication can doom the analyst and drive his listening to be ultimately superego driven. Needless to say that this problem is more likely to occur among candidates and those striving to become training analysts, since both these groups remain dependent upon third-party approval of technique.

To my mind, endless listening to repetitive material is a perversion of the analytic attitude. This should not be allowed to develop or continue for long. The pathological optimism and "someday . . ." fantasy (Akhtar, 1996) underlying the patient's repetition needs to be confronted and, in tenacious cases, ruptured. Basically, it comes down to "having to state that neither analysis nor analyst is an omnipotent rescuer, as the patients in their illusion needed to believe" (Amanti-Mehler and Argentieri, 1989, p. 301). The intervention is intended to inject "optimal disillusionment" (Gedo and Goldberg, 1973) in the clinical interaction and demands that the analysand learn to give up magical thinking. The desperate object hunger and the unconscious sadism usually associated with such monotonous repetitions can only then come to surface. All this might be a bit traumatic to the patient but it might also constitute a turning point of the analytic process provided, of course, the analyst's holding functions are in place and the effect of such a confrontative intervention can be analyzed.

All in all, listening is good. Listening patiently for a long time is better. But listening forever to material that is all too familiar constitutes a collusion with the patients' sadomasochism and narcissism. Such listening is contrary to the purposes of psychoanalysis.

CONCLUDING REMARKS

What I have offered here constitutes a rather cursory and heuristically modest overview of the topic of listening. I have explicated the developmental origins of the capacity to listen, locating them in the comfort with one's infantile receptive self, peaceful integration of maternal identifications, and successful renunciation of manic defense. I have delineated the specific characteristics of psychoanalytic listening and noted that it is an optimal blend of credulousness and skepticism; oscillations between these two poles occur in accordance with the patient's level of structural organization (Killingmo, 1989) and his or her capacity to retain psychological-mindedness and therapeutic alliance. Following this, I have highlighted the impact of characterological resistances, conceptual rigidity, countertransference blocks, and cultural differences within the dyad upon the analyst's capacity to listen. I have also touched upon the superego and id-induced perversions of analytic listening and noted the occasions where active and openly acknowledged 'not-listening' might be the correct technical stance. By way of doing all this, I have sought to modestly extend our knowledge in the realm of psychoanalytic listening.

The importance of listening though goes far beyond the clinical dialogue intended to relieve personal suffering. In today's world that is riddled with ethnic strife, so-called religious wars, and terrorisms of the rich and the poor both, listening to each other has acquired paramount importance. Valuable contributions of psychoanalyst-political scientist Vamik Volkan (1997, 2004, 2006) address this issue in a most meaningful way and the reader will benefit by looking them up. I do, however, want to underscore the importance of listening in the psychopolitical realm by raising a seemingly straightforward question. What would have happened if, after the horrible events of September 11, 2001, President George Bush, instead of reacting with violence, had summoned the most significant Arab head of states, asked them the reasons for some Muslims having become so hateful toward the United States, and carefully listened to their responses?

REFERENCES

Abbasi, A. 2007. Who's side are you on?: Muslim analysts analyzing non-Muslim patients. In: *The Crescent and the Couch: Cross Currents between Islam and Psychoanalysis*, ed. S. Akhtar. New York: Other Press.

Akhtar, S. 1996. "Someday....." and "if only...." fantasies: pathological optimism and inordinate nostalgia as related forms of idealization. *Journal of American Psychoanalytic Association* 44: 723–753.

———. 1999. *Immigration and Identity: Turmoil, Treatment, and Transformation.* Northvale, NJ: Jason Aronson.

———. 2000. From schisms through synthesis to informed oscillation: an attempt at integrating some diverse aspects of psychoanalytic technique. *Psychoanalytic Quarterly* 69: 265–288.

———. 2006. Technical challenges faced by the immigrant analyst. *Psychoanalytic Quarterly* 75.

———. 2007. Muslims in the psychoanalytic world. In: *The Crescent and the Couch: Cross Currents between Islam and Psychoanalysis.* Ed. S. Akhtar. New York: Other Press.

Amati-Mehler, J. and S. Argentieri. 1989. Hope and hopelessness: a technical problem? *International Journal of Psychoanalysis* 70: 295–304.

Amati-Mehler, J., S. Argentieri, and J. Cansestri. 1993. *The Babel of the Unconscious: Mother Tongue and Foreign Languages in the Psychoanalytic Dimension,* trans. J. Whitelaw-Cucco. Madison, CT: International Universities Press.

Arlow, J. 1995. Stilted listening: psychoanalysis as discourse. *Psychoanalytic Quarterly* 64: 215–233.

Bribring, E. 1954. Psychoanalysis and dynamic psychotherapies. *Journal of the American Psychoanalytic Association* 2: 745–770.

Breuer, J. and S. Freud. 1893–1895. Studies on hysteria. *Standard Edition* 2.

Freud, S. 1910. The future prospects of psycho-analytic therapy. *Standard Edition* 11: 139–151.

———. 1912. Recommendations to physicians practicing psychoanalysis. *Standard Edition* 12: 111–120.

———. 1913. On beginning the treatment. *Standard Edition* 12: 123–144.

Gedo, J. E. and A. Goldberg. 1973. *Models of the Mind.* Chicago: University of Chicago Press.

Gorkin, M. 1996. Countertransference in cross-cultural psychotherapy. In *Reaching across Boundaries of Culture and Class,* eds. R. Perez-Foster, M. Moskowitz, and R. A. Javier, pp. 47–70. Northvale, NJ: Jason Aronson.

Greenspan, S. I. 1977. The oedipal-preoedipal dilemma: a reformulation in the light of object relations theory. *International Review of Psychoanalysis* 4: 381–391.

Herzog, J. 1984. Fathers and young children: fathering daughters and fathering sons. In: *Foundations of Infant Psychiatry, Vol. 2,* eds. J.D. Call, E. Galenson, and R. Tyson, pp. 335–343. New York: Basic Books.

Killingmo, B. 1989. Conflict and deficit: implications for technique. *International Journal of Psychoanalysis.*

Klauber, J. 1968. The psychoanalyst as a person. *Difficulties in the Analytic Encounter*, pp. 123–139. New York: Jason Aronson.

Klein, M. 1935. A contribution to the psychogenesis of manic/depressive states. In: *Love, Guilt, and Reparation*, pp. 344–369. London: Hogarth, 1975.

Olinick, S. 1969. On empathy and regression in the service of the other. *British Journal of Medical Psychology* 42: 41–49.

Pine, F. 1988. The four psychologies of psychoanalysis and their place in clinical work. *Journal of the American Psychoanalytic Association* 36: 571–596.

Racker, H. 1968. Transference and Countertransference. London: Hogarth Press.

Roland, A. 1996. *Cultural Pluralism and Psychoanalysis: The Asian and North American Experience.* New York: Routledge.

Schwaber, E. 1998. From whose point of view? The neglected question in analytic listening. *Psychoanalytic Quarterly* 67: 645–661.

Spencer, J. H. and L. Balter. 1990. Psychoanalytic observation. *Journal of the American Psychoanalytic Association* 38: 393–421.

Strenger, C. 1989. The classic and romantic visions in psychoanalysis. *International Journal of Psychoanalysis* 70: 595–610.

Volkan, V. 1997. *Bloodlines: From Ethnic Pride to Ethnic Terrorism.* New York: Farrar, Straus, and Giroux.

———. 2004. *Blind Trust: Large Groups and Their Leaders in Times of Crises and Terror.* Charlottesville, VA: Pitchstone Publishing.

———. 2006. *Killing in the Name of Identity: A Study of Bloody Conflicts.* Charlottesville, VA: Pitchstone Publishing.

Winnicott, D. W. 1935. The manic defense. In: *Through Paediatrics to Psychoanalysis: Collected Papers*, pp. 129–144. New York: Brunner/Mazel, 1992.

———. 1960. The theory of a parent-infant relationship. *International Journal of Psychoanalysis* 41: 585–595.

Wright, K. 1991. *Vision and Separation: Between Mother and Baby.* Northvale, NJ: Jason Aronson.

2

The Unending Struggle to Listen

Locating Oneself within the Other

Evelyne Albrecht Schwaber, M.D.

Margaret Mahler's extraordinary contributions to infant observation and its link to the understanding of psychic life throughout the life span revolutionized our ways of thinking about development and about what we can know or learn in listening to our patients. Sparking ongoing innovation and symposia,[1] discussion and debate, psychoanalytic inquiry opened up to new terrains, as the clinician and the infant observer had more compellingly and profoundly to engage each other's findings and hypotheses. Dr. Mahler—whom I remember first hearing years ago, with a sense of awe, when I was a student at Einstein Medical School in the late 1950s—had stirred a vital, continuously generative step.

LISTENING WITH EMPATHY

I appreciate the opportunity to share some of my own views about how we, as clinicians, listen to another, and the difficulty, the struggle in that endeavor. The influence of infant observation, I believe, has sharpened our awareness and capacity to locate multiple levels of complexity in communication. Working as Consultant to the Pediatric service at Boston City Hospital in the 1960s, I called upon Louis Sander, who was doing his ground-breaking research there at the time, seeking his guidance with an infant failing to thrive. Sander's finely nuanced work on neonatal round-the-clock state monitoring, determining his life-saving suggestions with this baby, was instrumental in catalyzing my own thoughts about development and clinical process, and the communicative power in elucidating nonverbal cues (Sander, 1975, 1992; Schwaber, 2002).

To cite a recent clinical instance: Some time back, when I was out of the country, a patient, prone to severe states of anxiety—particularly about medical concerns, and heightened when I'm away—left a message of panic on my voice mail. (I'd had someone covering for me, but I also checked it periodically.) Apparently, a routine medical exam had raised some questions necessitating more tests. I called back—it was after 1:00 A.M. my time, early evening hers (I had just gotten in; people around me were sleeping)—and left a message on her answering machine to convey my concern and my presence; though she had a number to reach me overseas, we understood she preferred to simply call my office line. In my message, I asked that she let me know the follow-up test results. She left a voice-mail the next day indicating the test was normal, and I called back to say I was glad for that, thanking her for letting me know. Soon thereafter, she left a message saying she would be away for a few days on my return (an unusual occurrence) to recover from the traumatic experience. When we then resumed our meetings, I noticed, though she was no longer panicked, she seemed affectively remote. We spoke of the fact that I wasn't there when the traumatic experience occurred; replicating her early history, she'd felt abandoned at a time of need, and so perhaps had to stay away in response. Though we could recognize this sequence, her reserved, 'held-back' tone persisted nonetheless. I noted and commented on a passing reference she made to my having sounded "cold" on the phone—distant. "Yes," she replied, as we began to see it was my tone of voice, even beyond my physical absence, that had evoked the sense of injury. Had I sounded warmer, the geographic distance might have been narrowed.

From my vantage point, it had been the middle of the night; I was tired and had to speak softly. Yet thinking of her, I had not wanted to delay my return call to the next day. I could feel now a defensive tug in me for the seeming lack of affective recognition of what I had offered— my availability when away, tired, in the wee hours of the night, and despite someone else covering for me. I tried to get past that tug and speak to the meaning *she gave* to my tone. (Note my use of the phrase, "she gave," which seems to imply a weighing of *other*—rather than simply *her*—meaning.) I hadn't quite entered the depth of her inner world.

Her sense of injury persisted; she seemed not to be able to get past it—affectively—no matter how rationally she could think otherwise. Eventually, her persistence became a wake-up call to me to the possibility that I hadn't quite 'gotten it.' Somehow, I had hoped for her to consider that the way I'd sounded on the phone need not have only one interpretation—that is, for her to *re*-consider. Perhaps this hope was for reasons of my own.

The fundamental legitimacy of the feeling of injury deriving from my seeming perfunctory or detached way of speaking on the phone needed to be recognized—not just intellectually by me, but felt deeply within me. (I needed to recognize *amae* with her, as illuminated by the Japanese psychoanalyst, Takeo Doi, describing a concept of early connectedness for which there is no equivalent English word (1989; 1993; 2005). And then, the patient could reopen the wound, as I could begin to discover within myself that my tone did betray my own affective distance. In my case, as then in hers, it was the tone, beyond the words, which made the difference and spoke to this difference.

A patient once told me, "Not recognizing the legitimacy of the hurt is a far worse hurt than the hurt itself."

The capacity for empathy with another does not grow by virtue of reason; it blossoms as the patient's early needs, and reachings, *however individually varied,* are responded to—not in a pro forma way, but in conveying a fundamental and *affective* awareness of their nature. (I emphasize this—that is, the uniqueness and individuality of each person; to paraphrase Sander's cautionary note, attention to our duality must not supplant that of our individuality.[2]) Gaining this basic recognition and inherent legitimization allows the patient to regard the other, to see the other without relinquishing or losing the vitality of herself. (We all know of babies who fail to thrive though the mother goes through the seemingly correct motions of nursing and caretaking.)[3]

Only when I could—that is, when I allowed myself to—fully 'get' the injury my patient experienced, did she begin to feel heard. Regaining an affective awareness of me, a connectedness to me, her tone eased, and in time, she could tell more of what had happened to her, and how I had missed that.

Empathy, (or, for that matter, *amae*) developmentally or clinically, cannot be a formalistic response. I recall a patient who would tell me when she felt I was "positioning" rather than truly seeing her perspective.

At a panel illuminating a self-psychological view—with its particular emphasis on empathy as a central modality—a case was presented of a woman having had only short-lived relationships, still searching for the man of her dreams. Recounting a session, the analyst stated:

> The patient became irritated when I commented that we should help her stay connected to her feelings so she doesn't break up with someone and then regret it. I didn't realize she felt I was pushing her until the following day, when she saw me as her mother (who'd 'pushed').
>
> PATIENT: "I didn't want to come today. I started not to like you. . . . Sometimes I think you think I should like guys I don't like."
>
> ANALYST: "I know you do. That's very interesting."
>
> PATIENT: "You might say I should give guys a chance. . . . But you know, that's how my mother is."

A critical moment in how we listen: The patient assigned a familiar meaning to the analyst's comment about helping her so "she doesn't break up with someone and then regret it," evoking the experience of her mother—i.e., the transference (—or perhaps the patient shifted away, to the mother). But was this meaning—feeling "pushed"—given the analyst's empathic intent, viewed as a projection, a distortion from which the analyst could stand apart and observe, or was it a perceptual experience (perhaps suggesting she settle for less than the man of her dreams), the inherent legitimacy of which was still to be found? "I know you do," the analyst had responded (when the patient said "You think I should like guys I don't"), but does she see why? Does she get its more profound logic, its legitimacy? Does she struggle to find that? If so, we are not told of such a search. And so, it was not clear that the analyst (or others in discussion) had 'gotten it.' 'Getting it' requires a level of recognition that may move (or jar) us more profoundly than what may feel to be an empathic response. Empathy as a mirroring or compassionate reflection does not yet tell us if the analyst 'gets it.' Something must shift within us—*a moment of discovery*—as we find what our patients see. If we struggle with this, understand transference in this way—a perception, perceptual experience, historically rooted, not a distortion, yet intrapsychic—I believe such a shift can occur.

THE QUESTION OF PROJECTIVE IDENTIFICATION

At the IPA Congress of 2005, in Rio, on the theme of "Trauma," I participated on a panel entitled, "Listening to Traumatic Situations." I spoke of an article published sometime before, entitled 'Projective Identification and Consciousness Alteration' by Cimino and Correale (2005). The authors posed the interesting notion that non-declarative memory (memory that had never been explicit) may be the repository of trauma. They suggested that these nondeclared elements may appear within state changes occurring *in the analyst* as a consequence of projective identification ("The patient actively, though unconsciously . . . brings about particular changes in the analyst's state" (p. 51); their thesis: The analyst (or therapist) experiences the traumatic effect the patient does not, which can then be put to exploratory benefit.

I have, for some time, questioned this construct of projective identification (Schwaber, 1996, 2005a). I'm troubled by the idea of its being an indicator within the therapist/analyst of unconscious motive within the patient. Requiring a leap of inference (if not of faith) about meaning yet unconscious to the patient, I believe it raises a serious epistemological concern—if unconscious, how can we know that? For we can only know what is unconscious in past tense, when it has reached awareness; before then, it is yet a hypothesis. Further, it risks minimizing the analyst's experience of autonomy and responsibility for his or her own responses; and, as an epistemological concern, I have not heard this concept applied analogously, or as diligently, as proceeding in the reverse direction—that is, to suggest that the patient's experience in the transference would be an expression of projective identification—with the analyst "unconsciously inducing" defended-against affective responses in the patient. For any psychic concept to gain clinical validity, would it not necessitate the potential for its equivalent expression on either side of the couch?

I emphasize, our task is to seek the inner world of the patient—I do not speak of an 'interpersonal' or 'intersubjective' view—yet we share a commonality of psychological expression, of psychic experience, even as our life history, defensive, and adaptive modalities may differ. How else can we claim to recognize the experience within our patients? Indeed, I believe it is the recognition—basically, the *discovery*—cognitively and affectively, of this resonance of similarity within ourselves—not a projection unconsciously placed there—which permits us entrée, experientially, to the depths of *the patient's psychic world*, the purview of our search.[4] Otherwise, we are at risk of using theoretical constructs, or prefixed assumptions, to keep at distance.

Though I would then question the notion, epistemologically, that we can infer meaning derived from the *analyst's* state changes regarding what is unconsciously *intended* by the patient, it is surely possible that the analyst may identify with certain affective experiences in the patient, outside the patient's awareness, but felt in the ambience nonetheless. I do further believe that the patient's state and its shifts (likely affecting us) may be communicators of traumatic experience not otherwise represented or symbolized, lying in the domain of nondeclarative or implicit memory (1998; 2005b).

A number of authors (Stern et al., 1998; Fonagy, 1999; Davis, 2001) have taken the position that such memory, not having ever been explicit (and thereby not formally repressed), lies outside the domain of verbalizable exploration and thereby of potential recovery. I have not found this to be the case. I have, rather, consistently noted that the patient's nonverbal expressions (state, affect shifts, pauses), brought to mutually observable and articulated focus within the immediacy of the clinical moment, can serve as vital cues to realms heretofore outside conscious awareness, beyond explicit memory. Explication of these nonverbal cues can significantly narrow the leaps of inference made regarding yet unconscious meaning. They offer, I believe, another "royal road."

And they may help us, when explored, to learn about ourselves. For we may find they convey a response to us—analyst or therapist—derived from some communication we made suggesting meaning we may not before have seen or known within ourselves. A patient's hesitant state, for example, might be stirred by what is felt as our nonresponsiveness—perhaps we were quiet when words were sought; perhaps our quiet had reasons bearing on us, still unbeknown to us. We might react to some themes more than others, some affect states, in some moments more than others—*for reasons of our own.* (I have described a patient whose tone would become ever so subtly agitated, which, when I *finally* asked about it so that she too could observe it, we came to see was evoked when feeling criticized, unfairly blamed in the world out there, or by me. For a long time, I had not recognized this link—for my focus had been on helping her see her tendency to 'externalize' (1998). Patients may observe our preferences, and respond in turn, often with a nonverbal cue alone to inform us. I've often found, for example, that when patients speak directly about us, or when they speak with added liveliness or intensity, we're more likely to have something to say; in their own ways, they may call their awareness of our predilection to our attention, if we heed them.[5]

I should say, with regard to the title given to the Rio panel, I do not listen *to* trauma, *to* traumatic experience, as such. Listening to my patient—trying to—I may learn of her or his trauma—whether manifest for all to see, or more subtle, insidious, perhaps the ambience itself, traumatic. To paraphrase Shengold (1989), souls too risk murder—if more slowly, less apparent, over time.

I think of a patient who told me, in her flat tone, she worries that if she complains or speaks of being sad, I'll be hurt—that it would hurt my feelings. Why is that? I wondered. Had she perhaps perceived some affective resonance in my response to her sadness? "In what way, hurt my feelings? I asked, "and why would that stop you?" Then I thought and said, "Do you mean, if hurt, it would be on *my* account, not for *you*?" "That idea," she replied, "that it would be for me, never even occurred to me!"—her tone shifting, now sounding stirred. "Besides, it would be presumptuous," she said, entering a new path. Throughout her life, she began to see, she had feared others' vulnerability and expectations in relation to her. She'd felt she had to "position" herself to meet them. She hadn't known a feeling that it was *for her* that others were sad if she was hurt or hurting. This wasn't something forgotten—but hadn't been ever seen as an option in the first place as I hadn't seen the lack of it (Schwaber, 2005b; pp. 797–798[6])

Noting the negation of her sadness in her tone, and trying to clarify her stated reluctance to express it—*without myself understanding it*—a more fleshed-out picture of her mother's apparent vulnerability to feeling bad about—and for—herself, came forward. Mother seemed to need protection against such feeling, and the patient sought protection from her mother's self-referential response. Whatever the added conflictual dimensions in her worry about hurting me, this idea—for her—*that had never occurred to her*, and that I hadn't known was absent when I asked, deepened and contextualized their elucidation. Implicit memory, newly recognized, emerging to view—a profound sense of a world unsafe for knowing, sharing, valuing her 'true self' as the central background ambience. (A question aside: How might such an early mother-child interaction present itself to the infant observer?)

Is there not a universal here? Do we not each have moments, as did my patient, when we dare not share our own pain lest it be experienced by the other as a failing of hers, or his, a narcissistic injury? And are there not moments when, as analyst or therapist, we may take a patient's expression of continued sad feelings as injuries to our own person, to our clinical skills —either position, as subject or object, hard to acknowledge within ourselves, but with which we might nonetheless resonate?

A CLINICAL ILLUSTRATION

So, speaking of a world unsafe—outer and inner—let me tell you of Mr. A (2005b): On September 24, 2001 (thirteen days after the September 11, 2001, terrorist attacks), the *New Yorker* magazine, known for its often cogent, ironically metaphoric covers, featured a cover created by Art Spiegelman (the Pulitzer Prize-winning author of *Maus*, a comic strip narrative about the Holocaust). It was black, the entire page (except for the magazine's name and date) black. I looked again—actually, at first I didn't, but my patient invited me to look again. Beneath the black was another level of black—the Twin Towers of the World Trade Center. One had to look very closely, discerningly, to see it—its structure still present—deeply within the page's stark blackness. Spiegelman, it seemed, had once again evoked a powerful and understated piece of artistry depicting the horror. We might view this picture too as a metaphor to convey the subject of our work—the hidden and not so hidden, blackness.

I was setting out, at the time, to prepare a talk for a conference (on narcissism) on which I was to participate, first organized some months before. After September 11, I could no longer keep my focus on the task. I could feel and think only of the horror, obsessively reading all I could find about it, trying to reach some inner grounding. In order to write (in contrast, I should say, to listening to patients, which, with the human connection, I was able to do) I thought I would need to compartmentalize, dissociate perhaps. But I could not find a way to stay engaged, speaking from rational determination alone; for me, expressing ideas to paper, head and heart must come together. How, I thought, do we reconcile the effort to deal with events of such global enormity with a sustaining focus on subtle psychoanalytic themes? I speak of listening to nuance, miniscule shifts in affect and state in the psychic life of one individual; how does that matter now, I pondered?

Searching for meaning, maintaining some sense of relevance and truth in who we are, in what we do and feel, our smallness against the vastness beyond us—'how does that matter now?,' an age-old, existential question, may be a ubiquitous concern, perhaps too, a defense in the face of the larger trauma surrounding us (perhaps germane to the theme of narcissism, I thought). It might also be the struggle of the survivor's child. My patient helped me consider it.

Mr. A's maternal grandparents were killed as Jews, in the Holocaust. His mother had been transported to England as a teenager, and after the war, coming to the United States, changed her religion, married, had children, became active in her community, and never spoke of the truth of her identity or past. His father, American-born, also had suffered violent, though accidental, and unspoken loss, and had relinquished his Jewish identity. The patient—a brilliant and imaginative architect, pragmatic, very well-mannered, and in many ways, disconnected—learned not to ask, not even to wonder. It did not seem he even knew of a question he dared not ask. Rather, he was what he referred to as "clueless." He had long since learned to do what I could not at this time—draw a line against the pain, complete the task.

Life moved on for him in seeming comfort; he felt cared for—though feelings were neither expressed nor even noted—and he became quite accomplished. Some time after he went off to college, his mother committed suicide. He didn't understand; she'd had some earlier depression, but he could not integrate this occurrence. Overwhelmed, intellectually paralyzed, alarmed lest he fail his college requirements, he took a determined stance to put it all away, draw a line, do the task. And in the course of his analysis, despite efforts (perhaps mine more so than his) to bring it forward, this history as well as the state of mind that preceded it, remained beyond focus or affective connection.

One day, in late September 2001, he came in saying, with newly expressed intensity: "Did you see the cover of the *New Yorker*? It's a stunning piece of art, so powerful. . . . It's how I visualize my mom, black on black. The cover, you can't really see the World Trade Center, only in certain light, but it's indelibly there. *That picture captures what I've been struggling with all these years!*" And so it began to capture his struggle for me—his first expression of the notion of 'struggle.' (Some time later we learned of how the cover captured a more profound sense of "looking back for mother," of how hard his search to see her.)

Sometimes art, as with poetry, or music, can reach us, touch us, in ways we otherwise cannot quite grasp. We may have experienced this especially in those acutely difficult days. In a *New Yorker* article, John Lahr wrote, "In dark times, art can raise the pulse and lift the heart of a community" (Nov. 5, 2001). In another piece, Alex Ross wrote on the power of music (Oct. 8, 2001). He told of Wallace Stevens asking, during World War II, quoting Shakespeare, "How with this rage shall beauty hold a plea?" "How, in other words," Ross suggests, "can artists respond to news that exceed their most extravagant nightmares?" Stevens answers, artists "help us to live our lives," and the best they have to give is a certain quality of nobility, which he defined as "a violence from within that protects us from a violence without." My isolated, disconnected patient had often sought comfort in music. It is what moves him. He finds—he *feels* within it—a profound resonance—"a sense of power"; adding later, "like the feeling of my mother behind me." This time he found it, *found himself* (his mother perhaps), in a work of art on the cover of the *New Yorker*. And I could recognize and speak with him of it. And he found words.

He went on in that hour of plans to go to an event in downtown Boston but warnings were out of terror risks in town. He wondered whether his concern was rational; then he became quiet. I remarked on the quiet—his silent state shift. "My mind drifted off," he said, "not sure where," now looking at the moment. Then he noticed he'd had a fleeting thought about wanting to know if I too share that fear of going downtown, but didn't dare ask. That's when he became silent. He noticed, that is, that he'd had a question he wouldn't ask—what *I felt.* It "wouldn't be polite, anyway," he said. 'About me? About my fears?' (I wondered.) Not for him to touch upon. He'd squelched the question from his own awareness, noting, after I asked about the quiet, that his mind had wandered. He hadn't known these thoughts before—neither the question nor his fear of asking. Implicit, they lay in the realm of the nonverbal. Now he became aware, experientially, how he doesn't expect answers about such feelings, doesn't even know to seek them—that is, some communication from me that would allow him to know me and thereby himself—a step, we may consider, in the development of empathy. Besides, the feelings themselves are too dark—his, too insignificant in the face of the vast horror out there ("How does it matter now?")—to bear.

As I now glance back at this moment in the hour, after expressing his concern about a terror attack (in Boston) he had drifted into silence. I too had been silent. I, perhaps adrift between the potential for violence without and terror within (perhaps in some ways, like his parents) had said nothing of his concern, while he may have been, unknowingly, searching for some response, which had not come. I'd moved back *for reasons of my own,* perhaps in resonance with him—which I found only in noting his *subsequent* drift away. And so, the blackness behind the blackness had once again receded. *The analyst's silence may equally intrude into the patient's associative stream, as can her words; our silence too is a communication.* (In other words, we no more interrupt by speaking than by saying nothing. Each mode may derive meaning.)

Listening to our patient, open-endedly, without knowing, hearing the trauma within and without—'getting it,' is difficult. In these darker days, perhaps it has become more so. The *New Yorker* picture, stirring him, helped me see that. It made me think of other aspects of his experience I hadn't heard (or hadn't seen, for as in the picture, that could only occur in certain light), and of how he'd informed me of that.

As I'd indicated, Mr. A., despite his professional accomplishments, had felt himself, in ordinary social interaction, as in the analysis, to be "clueless" (cf., pp. 798–803). From the outset of our work together (though he'd had prior therapy), he felt he didn't understand—neither psychic process, nor irrational thinking, nor did he get the idea of defense. He didn't "get" that there were multiple levels of complexity about his past or in human relatedness, that these are not one-dimensional, linear matters. This state of fundamental "cluelessness" seemed to me profoundly interwoven with the family's inability to tell, to speak, to open a space for him to ask (of matters sexual as well as historical and emotional). But he too was afraid, I thought—perhaps not just to ask, but to know. I tried to help him consider this, to see the workings of his mind, to point to some seemingly (to me) 'obvious' defensiveness in his stream of associations, or in the detached way he recounts his poignant history; I tried to help him see what he could not, where his feelings 'really' lie, and his fear of them. And he seemed to 'get it'—that is, what I was conveying.

I began to notice, he didn't look at me when leaving at the hour's end. That is, I began to allow myself to see that.

In ensuing sessions, he spoke of feeling he's fallen short—his mind not making the connections or responding as it "should have," unable to do what he "ought to" in analysis. His tone sounded more detached (—at least, I began to observe that).

The turn in his glance, shift in his tone, carried nonverbal cues to what I might not otherwise have noted—an inner voice not being heard, possibly going underground. It seemed that trying to help him get it, I too, now reflecting, had been trying to keep on the 'task.' I had not been listening to what it feels like in *his* shoes. He'd said he didn't have a "clue," and in my apparent effort to provide it, I turned away from learning just what that feeling is. Neither he nor I recognized this turn. But I then found it—the paradox of my pulling away by seeming to move toward—not by first discovering it within myself, but by listening to him. ("Something is happening that makes you feel you're not doing this right," to paraphrase myself; "I'm clueless," he reiterated and with the added detached emphasis, I finally heard.) Catching hold of the disconnection in his look and in his tone, I began to see, shifting my stance, how I had joined him—*no, not joined him; he, though afraid, also wanted to know*. Perhaps I did not; perhaps I held back from the depth of his overwhelming terror and affective isolation—the history of his life, then and now—and its vast unarticulated burden. Silently, he had unflinchingly, to keep using his exceptional talents and intellect for the six million lost who could not use theirs, and for his mother. Feelings and history he didn't know he had, unresponded to, unexpressed, now emerging.

> If to remember is to provide the disembodied 'wound' with a psychic residence then to remember other people's memories is to be wounded by their wounds. More precisely, to let the traces of other people's struggles, passions, past, resonate within one's own past and present, and destabilize them. (Silverman, 1996, p. 189).

I would then reiterate: I was not aware of any *untoward* pull in me to provide a clue, but to help him find the workings of his mind. (My analytic efforts felt ego-syntonic to me.) I do not know that I could have relied on myself to discover such a pull—at least not at that time—and though his manner may have evoked it in me, we found no basis for saying he unconsciously "put" or projected it into me. Even if responding to his defensive stance—perhaps swept along by it—the reasons keeping me from moving closer to the depth of his feelings were *my own*. We did not learn of any hidden motive on his part to keep me away; on the contrary, as we saw, *he felt worse when I did so*. (When the patient's pain and trauma are especially poignant, we may find ourselves more likely to shift back to psychoanalytic "principles," to guide, reinforcing his defenses, perhaps wishing to spare him as well as ourselves.) The entry into Mr. A's experience came with the observation of *his* nonverbal and verbal cues—the look away, the detached tone, the feeling he's falling short—and heeding them. And so we learned how his perception of me, of *my* way of being, *my* efforts, evoked a historic resonance within him—the background sense of his feelings of loss, untethered, bypassed—*as newly recovered implicit memory*. His transference—by its definition—was seen to bear the inclusion of his perception, his perceptual experience.

It is always difficult to listen—without foreclosure, to follow the course, to learn what we hadn't before seen. We are inclined, wittingly or not, however subtly, to guide, to help the patient see hidden meaning we believe we already see, leaving aside the opportunity to learn that we do not (and thereby to bring what has been unconscious forward). It wasn't that I ought not to have asked if he's afraid to know, that is, to consider a defense in the not knowing—I need not squelch my own wonderings—but it was my position when I did so, not truly one of inquiry, with which I needed to reckon. Listening, as Corradi Fiumara (1990) notes, demands our "vulnerability," our "totality." The struggle to listen—the unending struggle—I would add, demands a central shift in our sense of knowing another's inner meaning, calling upon our capacity for resonance, to find within ourselves—with our patient's help—the conflictual, shameful, painful, even heartbreaking commonality in our experience, our ways of being, and of defending. How much more so when the motifs are immersed within the background of trauma. (Mr. A. could not even speak the words of violence or of sex.)

CODA

One day, after prolonged deliberation, Mr. A decided to go to visit his mother's birthplace and surroundings, try to learn more of her and thereby of his history. "I'm doing this in her memory," he said, "an honoring way. She didn't. I'm just a proxy. She should have gone back to see it. If she were alive, I'd try to talk her into it; maybe there'd be some way to be at peace about it." "And not have to kill herself," I said. "Yeah!" he responded. "Could there be some other way to come to peace with it, to see it—as part of her life—and not have to cut off from it?" With trepidation, he was going, so he might see it, *see her*, as part of his life (—one might consider, his seeking an empathic recognition of her).

Recognition—articulated by another and oneself, linking past, newly found, to present—as the mode of therapeutic action. Recognition, 'getting it,' holding the central developmental thrust, as Sander (1992) has compellingly articulated—and the clinical thrust, as noted by Doi (1993).[7] Recognition—thereby allowing the emergence of the fuller affective sense of the experience of the trauma—of the buried, implicitly remembered, nondeclared *ambience* in which Mr. A had lived, of the loss of his mother and of his mother's loss. One day, beginning to take in my schedule changes when they occurred (about which he'd been 'clueless'), he said, "I'm aware that with the time changes, you're away for the Jewish holidays (not something I had explicitly said). It's a double loss; it's a part of me that's missing, that I've never known." "Known but not known," I said. "Yes, it's an interesting thing, that you're away for the holidays—I like that. It's an honoring thing, like my using my father's pen, or like my putting the stones on my relatives' graves in Germany. I do feel there's something I've got to do; there's something I owe those people who perished." "So you feel some comfort in my carrying on their tradition," I said. "Yeah! … I feel like I've abandoned them, so I do appreciate your showing up in that regard."

Another patient once told me, "When you hear the way my mind works without saying it should work another way, that lets me experience more about how my mind works—and *to remember more* (the shame, the terror, the chaos)."[8]

"Hear the way my mind works without saying it should work another way"—a profound lesson, repeatedly eluding us, yet, as we struggle toward it, offering us the extraordinary opportunity for a deepening, if unsettling venture and discovery.

"Clueless" was the way Mr. A's mind worked. I tried to have it work another way. But when I did not, he experienced more about how his mind works, and remembered more. As I needed him to show me the blackness behind, I needed too, to listen, to hear him tell me, so that I could "get it" and find in me—what it is like to live in "clueless" (and the fear of emerging from it).

"I feel sometimes," he told me on returning from Germany, "as if I was dropped out of the sky, with nothing to tell me who I am. . . . But now I feel like I understand my connection to that family." (That is, we might paraphrase, "I have developed empathy for that connection. I 'get it.'") "Clueless" was having felt dropped out of the sky, a sensation, a state, a meaning not before articulated—memory nondeclared, implicit, recovered—perhaps another image we might implicitly envision in the New Yorker cover.

An afterthought: Some time back, I came upon a book by the American author M. R. Montgomery (1989) written about his father, who was away in the service when he was a child. There is a stirring passage in this book which I would like again to cite:

> There is this thing that happens with children: If no one is watching them, nothing is really happening to them. It is not some philosophical conundrum like the one about the tree falling in the forest and no one hearing it; that is a puzzler for college freshmen. No. If you are very small, you actually understand that there is no point in jumping into the swimming pool unless they see you do it. The child crying, 'Watch me, watch me,' is not begging for attention; he is pleading for existence itself. They will remember. They will hold it, keep it, make it true. Everything else is dreams, not memories. This is what I would have told my father, about 1942 and 1943, when he was gone. (p. 143)

A Kantian point: The tree in the forest must be seen to exist. To watch, to listen, to recognize, "getting it"—a 'moment of meeting,' an expression of *amae*—perhaps it may be seen as a granting of existence itself.

Notes

1. Including today's event which is titled "Listening to Others: Clinical and Developmental Aspects of Empathy and Attunement." This rich and multilayered title raises an implicit question: Are we speaking of empathy for developmental

aspects, or of developmental aspects in attainment of the capacity for empathy—in the child, in the patient, or in the clinician?

2. "From the cell upward, living organisms are actively self-regulating and, at the same time, of necessity exist in a continuous intimate exchange with essential support factors provided by the surround. There is an obvious polarity inherent in this view; attention to either cannot be given at the expense of the other" (Sander, 1975, pp. 134–135).

3. I had originally envisaged this necessity for recognition as in keeping with the development of the child's capacity for empathy. However, on further reflection on my own clinical experience, it occurred to me that the developmental aspects of empathy may be more complex, with vicissitudes not fully analogous to those seen in the progression of clinical work. (In discussion with Dr. Sander, he concurred that this is a subject warranting further research.) I think of a patient, for example, who was affectively quite deprived as a child, yet grew to attain an extraordinary empathic gift, long before she ever came to treatment. Reflecting on this occurrence, I have wondered whether her growing up in the deep South, witness to the apparent degradation of the black people, may have nurtured this facility, perhaps in some identification. She herself, noting her genuine capacity for "lovingness" with others (which in no way negates, rather, enriches the range of other more conflictual or 'negative' feelings), saw it as offering her "light;" that is, this emotion keeping her psychically alive. It made me think again of Doi's work on *amae,* perhaps resonating with such a view—and marking a striking cross-cultural bridge. In *My Traitor's Heart,* about his attachment to his native South Africa, Rian Malan evokes a poetic allusion to this theme: "I realized that love, even if it ends in defeat, gives you a kind of honor; but without love, you have no honor at all…love is to enable you to transcend defeat….The only thing you can do is love, because it is the only thing that leaves light inside you, instead of the total, obliterating darkness" (1991; p. 409). My patient, telling me of this book, brought my attention to this passage.

4. Doi: "Only those who are aware (or, I would add, who become aware) of the hidden need within themselves are alert to the same need in others." Personal communication.

5. Elsewhere (1995), I wrote of an analysis that seemed to be going quite well—with apparent deepening material, dreams, fantasies emerging, resistances uncovered—until I paid heed to the quieter cues. It appeared that the patient became more energized just after my comments, a shift in state about which I then asked him. Now observing this, he reflected that he felt my words had been "recharging" him, giving him—and me as well— a feeling that he was "with" me. His response, I had to recognize, energized me too. It seemed it was less the con-

tent of my interventions, than the fact of my making them that held the decisive import. Both of us had been going along in what we came to see as our "analytic dance." Only as this silent dimension of his experience was uncovered (and for that I had to ask about what I did not know and find what I had not before seen in myself), did something more fundamental to who he was and more powerfully defended become illuminated.

6. In Oliver Sacks's (1985) essay on twin idiot savants, autistic numerical geniuses, he discovers, after closely observing them, their striking joy in playing certain extraordinary number games with each other that they seemed uniquely to comprehend. Studying this, he recognized the game was of guessing primes, and he then located some especially difficult numbers for them to guess. They then saw that he 'got' it, and so began to include him in their joyful game. He wrote: "They see, directly, a universe and heaven of numbers. And this, however singular, however bizarre—but what right have we to call it 'pathological'?—provides a singular self-sufficiency to their lives, and one which it might be tragic to interfere with, or break." But eventually, the twins were separated, in order, apparently, to help them adapt more ably to the world. They learned to hold menial jobs and keep themselves moderately presentable and clean, which was considered a central gain. But, Sacks writes, the "negative side" was "not mentioned in their charts, because *it was never recognized in the first place* (my emphasis). Deprived of their numerical 'communion' with each other, and of time and opportunity for any 'contemplation'...they seem to have lost their strange numerical power, and with this the chief joy and sense of their lives. But this is considered a small price to pay, no doubt, for their having become quasi-independent and 'socially acceptable'" (p. 199).

7. Sander (1992) describes "a moment of specificity in recognition, when the child becomes aware that another is aware of what he is aware of within himself. This is a specificity in an experience of meeting that brings a moment of new coherence to the child's awareness of both the inner and the outer....if the moment of 'being known' was reached, there ensues a change in the child's self-regulatory organization that endures over many years, even (if) from just one experience. It is this process of specificity in recurrent moments of meeting that I have referred to as recognition process, and have proposed it as basic to at least four domains of ongoing process in living systems: the biological, the negotiation of adaptive issues in early development, the construction of continuity over the life span, and the therapeutic process" (p. 583). Doi (1993) speaks of this specificity in the clinical instance. Commenting on a case report of mine, when it appeared I had 'gotten it,' that is, my patient's meaning, Doi notes, "It means he understood that she understood what he really meant to say. And that in itself

was good enough, because what he was really hoping for was not a hug itself (as he'd said he wished for) but to be understood in the depth of his mind" (p. 169). Mr. A spoke of a similar experience with his daughter, who learned to play a piece on the piano that had great meaning to him. "She played it so beautifully," he said. "She practiced it so diligently. She 'got it!' So I know that she knew how important that was to me, and that was a sharing because of that."

8. In his remarks on my presentation this chapter, Sydney Pulver (in this volume) asked what happens next when I 'get it?' In his words: "Once we get it, how do we carry it to the patient?" Here I would respond, citing Doi and Sander: "He understood that she understood what he really meant to say. And that in itself was good enough"; "A moment of 'being known' was reached," a moment of "new coherence," a change in "self-regulatory organization"; and, as this patient said, "That lets me experience more about how my mind works." That is, the search to 'get it' is the route, and the goal, enabling the therapeutic action.

REFERENCES

Cimino, C. and A. Correale. 2005. Projective identification and consciousness alteration. *International Journal of Psychoanalysis* 86: 51–60.

Corradi Fiumara, G. 1990. *The Other Side of Language: A Philosophy of Listening.* London: Routledge.

Davis, J. T. 2001. Revising psychoanalytic interpretations of the past: an examination of declarative and non-declarative memory processes. *International Journal of Psychoanalysis* 82: 449–462.

Doi, T. 1989. The concept of *amae* and its psychoanalytic implications. *International Review of Psychoanalysis* 16: 349–354.

———. 1993. *Amae* and transference-love. In: *On Freud's 'Observations on Transference-Love;'* ed. E. Person, A. Hagelin, and P. Fonagy, pp. 165–171. New Haven, CT: Yale University Press.

———. 2005. *Understanding Amae: The Japanese Concept of Need-Love.* Kent, UK: Global Oriental Ltd.

Fonagy, P. 1999. Memory and therapeutic action. *International Journal of Psychoanalysis* 80: 215–223.

———. 2003. Rejoinder to Harold Blum. *International Journal of Psychoanalysis* 84: 503–509.

Lahr, J. 2001. *The New Yorker*, Nov. 5.

Malan, M. 1991. *My Traitor's Heart.* London: Vintage.

Montgomery, M. R. 1989. *Saying Goodbye: A Memoir for Two Fathers.* New York: Knopf.

Ross, A. 2001. Requiems in the city. *New Yorker*, Oct. 8.

Sacks, O. 1985. The twins. In: *The Man Who Mistook His Wife for a Hat*, pp. 185–203. New York: Summit Books.

Sander, L. W. 1992. Letter to the Editor. *International Journal of Psychoanalysis* 73: 582–584.

———. 1975. Infant and caretaking environment: investigation and conceptualization of adaptive behavior in a system of increasing complexity. In: *Explorations in Child Psychiatry*, ed. E. J. Anthony. New York: Plenum.

Schwaber, E.A. 1995. The psychoanalyst's mind: from listening to interpretation—a clinical report. *International Journal of Psychoanalysis* 76: 271–281.

———. 1996. The conceptualization and communication of clinical facts in psychoanalysis: a discussion. *International Journal of Psychoanalysis* 77: 235–253.

———. 1998. The non-verbal dimension in psychoanalysis: 'state' and its clinical vicissitudes. *International Journal of Psychoanalysis* 79: 667–679.

———. 2002. Psychoanalysis at the millennium: a personal odyssey. *Psychoanalytic Inquiry* 22: 55–75.

———. 2005a. Letter to Editor in response to "Projective identification and consciousness alteration," by C. Cimino & A Correale. *International Journal of Psychoanalysis* 86: 900–901.

———. 2005b. The struggle to listen: continuing reflections, lingering paradoxes, and some thoughts on recovery of memory. *Journal of the American Psychoanalytic Association* 53: 789–810.

Shengold, L. 1989. *Soul Murder: The Effect of Child Abuse and Deprivation.* New Haven, CT: Yale University Press.

Spiegelman, A. 1996. *Maus: A Survivor's Tale.* New York: Pantheon.

Silverman, K. 1996. *The Threshold of the Visible World.* New York: Routledge.

Stern, D. et al. 1998. Non-interpretive mechanisms in psychoanalytic therapy: the something more than interpretation. *International Journal of Psychoanalysis* 79: 903–921.

3

'Getting It' and Knowing What to Do When One Does Not 'Get It'

Discussion of Schwaber's Chapter "The Unending Struggle to Listen: Locating Oneself within the Other"

Sydney E. Pulver, M.D.

Dr. Evelyne Schwaber has been a trailblazer in the world of analytic listening. Foreshadowed in her first paper (Schwaber, 1977), this interest came to the fore in her second (Schwaber, 1979), at which time she was heavily influenced by self psychology. With her classical paper "Empathy: A Mode of Analytic Listening" (Schwaber, 1981), she took the obscure phrase 'analytic listening' and made it a focus of analytic interest ever since. She was in at the beginning of a wave of analytic thought known as the relational turn, a reaction against the classical view of the analyst as an objective, unbiased observer. Relational psychoanalysis sees the analyst as a participant in the analytic process, indeed, as a co-constructor of that process.

Schwaber's main point in this and other papers is that we must listen to clinical material from the patient's viewpoint. She calls that 'getting it,' and I will also do so. In this discussion, I will make several points. First, I will wonder whether Schwaber, in spite of her own objections, cannot best be seen as a relational theorist. Second, I will point out that 'getting it' is only one aspect of the analyst's working stance. Third, I will describe the times during an analysis when it is particularly important for the analyst to 'get it.' Fourth, I will discuss why disruptions in the analytic relationship are so important, and finally, I will consider how such disruptions may be repaired.

SCHWABER AND RELATIONAL THEORY

Schwaber gives us several examples of clinical situations in which she finally 'gets it.' When she talks about the process involved, she usually describes the simple shifting of one's point of view from her own to that of the patient, a position which is often called a more empathic one. But what happens is more complex. When one looks at it in greater detail, one sees Schwaber shifting her entire stance with the patient, a shift quite typical of a relational position. She not only sees what the patient is feeling, but she comes to see her own role in the genesis of that feeling, and how she and the patient have been interacting to construct that feeling. Her first patient illustrates that nicely. Let's call her Mrs. X. Schwaber was away. Mrs. X left her a message and Schwaber returned her call. On a primary level, she returned the call because she genuinely cared about Mrs. X, and because she felt that it was important for the patient's well-being and for the continuation of the analysis that she respond. But she also responded (not quite consciously) to Mrs. X's pressure for her to be the always available, all caring mother, and at some level she knew that she could not and did not want to be. At some level, in addition to caring, we suspect she was also feeling something like "God damn it! It's 1:00 A.M. and I'm in Paris! Let me be!" Mrs. X sensed this, and the relationship was disrupted. Schwaber was ultimately able to see this from Mrs. X's point of view and to convey it. Only this mutual understanding could effect a repair.

I think that 'getting it,' as illustrated by this example, is an integral part of the relational therapeutic position. When a disruption occurs in any relationship of emotional importance, and certainly the analytic relationship meets that criterion, both partners play a role. Sometimes the role of the analyst has been relatively minor, thrust upon her mainly by the requirement of the analytic situation that she maintain the primary stance of trying to understand. But far more often, the principle of role responsiveness has been at work. The patient has not only wished for the analyst to play a transferential role, but has been actively attempting, in a variety of subtle or not so subtle ways, to pressure her to do so. Most of us believe these days that the analyst cannot avoid doing so to some extent. Hopefully, the analyst has been attempting to be aware of this tendency and her inevitable response, but it is only by being in it that she can detect it and try to make it clear to the patient. Analysis, most relational theorists would say, proceeds by a series of enactments and insight into those enactments. To achieve that understanding, Schwaber first had to understand it herself. She had to 'get it.' So, although Schwaber herself demurs, I believe she is advocating an essential principle of relational analysis, and illustrating it in a most eloquent and sensitive way.

'GETTING IT' IS ONLY ONE PART OF THE ANALYTIC STANCE

Whenever anyone writes a paper, they are trying to make a point. Schwaber is trying to impress on us the importance of listening from the patient's point of view. She is a gentle, eloquent, persuasive exponent, and it is easy to make the mistake of thinking that she is saying that this is the *only* mode of analytic listening. One might easily think that Schwaber is advocating that the analyst should consciously and intentionally be working with 'getting it' in mind. In following her work over the years, it is obvious that many of her critics (e.g., Arlow, 1995) have made that mistake, and she has patiently and convincingly refuted them. Examples of other modes of listening are legion. One thinks of the even hovering attention of Freud (1912), the reverie of Ogden (1997), the "without memory or desire" stance of Bion (1967), and, of course, our quotidian daily cognitive theoretical puzzling about what the patient is trying to say. Schwaber obviously knows all of this, so why the emphasis on the patient's point of view? Don't all good analysts these days try, among other things, to 'get it'? I can't imagine anyone saying "No" to this question, but in practice, things aren't that ideal. Schwaber is trying to call our attention to the powerful human tendency, shared by analysts, to listen from our own point of view. We are pushed in that direction by many forces. Our scientific tradition is that of the objective observer. We tend to adhere to one 'school,' one theoretical approach, and that approach, of course, embodies our own point of view. The patient sees us as an expert (which, of course, in some ways we are), and expertise in most fields means seeing oneself as the final arbiter of what is going on. And finally, we share the tremendous human intolerance of uncertainty, and how best to counter it than with the certainty of our own point of view? But Schwaber is requiring us to *not know*, in order to be open to the patient's point of view. For all of these reasons, 'not getting it' is easy to do, and staying open to the patient's point of view requires constant advocacy.

To be fair, though, we must also realize that there are a lot of times when the analyst *does* get it. Schwaber tends, at times, to leap to the conclusion that she doesn't. Her discussion of the panel case presentation in which a patient objects that her analyst is pushing her implies that the analyst, while empathic, doesn't really get it. I would say that though, as she states, there is no evidence that the analyst, the panel, and the audience itself got it, there is no evidence that they didn't. The idea that getting it requires an internal struggle, the overcoming of the feeling of certainty in our own point of view, is not convincing. But Schwaber, I think, is just trying to illustrate how easy it is to look at things from our own point of view, and with that I totally agree.

WHEN IS 'GETTING IT' PARTICULARLY IMPORTANT?

It seems obvious that analysts should always be open to understanding the relationship from the patient's point of view. If we look at the vignettes that Schwaber describes in this and other papers, however, we see that they almost always describe a situation in which a disturbance has occurred in the patient-analyst relationship. This is not surprising; Greenberg (2001) has pointed it out as characteristic of many papers written to illustrate some aspect of technique in relational analysis. We're all familiar with such disturbances, though we may call them by a number of different terms: a failure of the working alliance, an empathic failure, a disruption of the relationship. They may be sudden and acute, or gradually developing. Such disruptions have many causes, one of the most frequent of which, in my experience, is the analyst's failure to see things from the patient's viewpoint. Schwaber's vignette about Mr. A is typical of the phenomenology. The patient usually is struggling to convey some aspect of his experience. The analyst is struggling to understand, and either remains silent or responds in a way which proves to be not quite on target. The patient feels misunderstood and hurt, and indicates this in any of an infinite number of ways. The analyst senses a disturbance, and continues his struggle to understand. At this point, the analyst's ability to look at things from the patient's point of view, to 'get it,' is of the essence. If the analyst, under the impact of the uncertainty and uneasiness which disruptions like this always evoke, falls back on analyst-centered interpretations, the disruption is likely to continue. Understanding in terms of genetics and defense, so useful most of the time, are not reparative here. It is true that many patients can tolerate our everyday failure to understand, set it aside for the time being, and continue working. But a steady diet of this, and for some, even a small spoonful, will block analytic process until the rupture is repaired.

DISRUPTIONS OF THE ANALYTIC RELATIONSHIP

Their importance

One of the most salient issues suggested by the pluralism in psychoanalysis today is the question of common ground (Wallerstein, 1990). At least part of that common ground is suggested by the simple observation that most of the case vignettes in the psychoanalytic literature, regardless of the school to which the author adheres, have one of two purposes. They either advance various ways of understanding our patients' dynamics, or they describe ways of dealing with disruptions in the analytic relationship. These disruptions capture the attention of analysts of many schools. The reason for their importance may seem obvious, but let's spell it out.

Psychoanalysis can be viewed as a very special kind of human relationship. There are many kinds of relationships, and they exist for many purposes. The analytic relationship is special in that it is the only one in which the ultimate aim is to understand what is going on between the two participants. Other aims, such as therapeutic, of course exist, but I believe that understanding is the overarching aim, common to analysts of all schools. The basic background of a successful analysis is the same as the basic background of any successful relationship: a feeling of mutual understanding. This feeling isn't necessarily continuous, or uniform or present at all times. But it must be present enough of the time so that each individual feels that if the understanding is disrupted, it can be repaired. This, of course, is old hat, and has been talked about under many different names: basic trust, the analytic attitude, mutuality, the unobjectionable positive transference, and so on. It relates also to the newer things we are talking about these days, such as mentalization. To mentalize is to hold in one's mind the realization that the other has a mind of his own, with his own feelings, thoughts, and intentions. One cannot feel understood without recognizing that the person who understands you has you in his mind. You must, that is, be able to mentalize, and you must be able to sense that the person with whom you are interacting can mentalize. But there are yet other dimensions to understanding and feeling understood, as we are using those terms. To feel understood, you must have the feeling that your partner views you with at least some positive feeling, and is not viewing you either negatively or with disinterest. And finally, you must feel that he senses that the two of you are having an impact on each other, and that he is willing to assume responsibility for his part in the interaction. The above is idyllic, but I think it captures the main ingredients of what we hope for in a good relationship. We don't work well with people with whom we have a bad relationship, so it is essential that disruptions be attended to. This leads to our next point.

Ways to repair them

Psychoanalytic interaction can be thought of as a special kind of conversation (see Arlow 1995 for a discussion of this). Like all human communication, all conversations are characterized by misunderstandings and clarifications. In keeping with the recent relational literature (see, for instance, Benjamin's chapter in this volume), we have been calling these 'disruptions' and 'repairs.' Conversations progress toward a successful conclusion as long as both of the partners in the relationship are able to maintain a feeling that ultimately, if not right at the moment, the other will be able to understand, will be able to 'get it.' We don't need them to agree, but they must at least be able to understand. Small misunderstandings are tolerable. They do not necessarily wipe out the hope of being understood, and they are accompanied by repeated attempts to get one's feelings across. Major misunderstandings destroy for the moment the hope of being understood, and lead to a disruption in the relationship.

And now for our question: When a disruption occurs in analysis, how can the analyst help to repair it? At this point, our view of the analytic relationship becomes all important. If we view the analysis as something taking place mainly within the patient, we are in difficulty. If we see it as taking place in the interaction, as something generated between the two of us, with each of us having a role in what is taking place, our sailing is smoother. I venture here to be apodictic: When an analyst recognizes that a disruption has taken place, he should *always* wonder about what part he has played in bringing about the misunderstanding. He will be wondering about a myriad of other things as well, but his own role in the interaction must be one of them. The patient feels misunderstood and is hurt. Not recognizing the legitimacy of such a feeling is a far greater hurt than the original misunderstanding itself. This, I think, is what Schwaber has been telling us about seeing things from the patient's viewpoint, about the first step in the repair of a disruption, 'getting it.'

Once we 'get it,' how do we convey it to the patient? Some astute clinicians (e.g., Edgar Levenson, quoted in Hirsch and Iannuzzi, 2005) feel that there is no need to even make the attempt, that 'getting it' is enough. Most of us, I think, simply try, in ordinary words, to let the patient know how we understand things. By and large, that will be enough. The disruption will be repaired, and work will go on in a more harmonious manner until the next inevitable disruption. But let us not be naïve. We all know that many disruptions are not repaired so easily. That leads to a wealth of other considerations and questions and I shall but list a few of them:

1. Have we really gotten it? Do we really see our role in it? Are we being blocked by our own conflicts? Do we need a consultation, or, God forbid, more analysis?
2. Are the simple, ordinary words we've used enough? How can we get it across more affectively? What is the role of self-disclosure in doing so? Is some kind of more affective communication on our part needed? If so, what? Can we do it?
3. Should we wonder more deeply about the dynamics that are keeping the patient from feeling understood? This is the realm of the negative therapeutic reaction, the destruction of the analyst's mind so eloquently described by Joseph (1983), the inability to mentalize, and a host of other dynamics described at some point by one or another of the analytic schools.

CONCLUSION

In conclusion, I want to thank Evie Schwaber for the advice she has given us on analytic listening today and over the years. I agree with her about what I think has been her main point: No understanding of dynamics will be helpful if the analyst does not have the orientation and the ability to recognize that he is a participating member in the analytic duo, that he plays some part in the patient's reaction to him, and that he must not only recognize that, but be able to communicate it in some meaningful way to the patient. Above all, he first has to 'get it.'

REFERENCES

Arlow, J. A. 1995. Stilted listening: psychoanalysis as discourse. *Psychoanalytic Quarterly* 64: 215–233.

Bion, W. 1967. Notes on memory and desire. *Psychoanalytic Forum* 2: 271–280.

Greenberg, J. 2001. The analyst's participation. *Journal of the American Psychoanalytic Association* 49: 359–381.

Freud, S. 1912. Recommendations to physicians practicing psychoanalysis. *Standard Edition* 12: 111–120.

Hirsch, I. and V. P. Iannuzzi. 2005. Interview with Edgar Levinson. *Journal of Contemporary Psychoanalysis* 41: 320–331.

Joseph, B. 1983. On understanding and not understanding: some technical issues. *International Journal of Psychoanalysis* 64: 291–298.

Ogden, T. H. 1997. Reverie and interpretation. *Psychoanalytic Quarterly* 66: 567–595

Schwaber, E. 1977. 'You are my standard of time . . . a winged victory holding a clock. . .': an evolving understanding of an unfolding 'narcissistic transference. *International Review of Psychoanalysis* 4: 493–502.

———. 1979. On the 'self' within the matrix of analytic theory—some clinical reflections and reconsiderations. *International Journal of Psychoanalysis* 60: 467–479.

———. 1981. Empathy: a mode of analytic listening. *Psychoanalytic Inquiry* 1: 357–392.

———. 1992. Countertransference: the analyst's retreat from the patient's vantage point. *International Journal of Psychoanalysis* 73: 349–361.

———. 1998. From whose point of view? the neglected question in analytic listening. *Psychoanalytic Quarterly* 67: 645–661.

Wallerstein, R. S. 1990. Psychoanalysis: the common ground. *International Journal of Psychoanalysis* 71: 3–20.

4

LISTENING TOGETHER

Intersubjective Aspects of the Analytic Process of Losing and Restoring Recognition

Jessica Benjamin, Ph.D.

Facing the task of writing about listening I immediately found myself having an association to one of our family routines when my children were young, which involved them looking for some lost or misplaced object and being unable to find it. Their father would then find it exactly in the place they had been looking, saying "You have to know how to look." As we recently revisited that familiar experience I considered the meaning of that phrase, which implied not only that it was necessary to think about where to look, but also to *see* what you were looking at. Likewise, I thought, it is necessary to *hear* what you are listening to. Just as in Poe's story of "The Purloined Letter," which Lacan (1977) famously wrote about, in which the story turns on the experience of putting something in a place where others see but don't see it. In this chapter I suggest some thoughts about the ever-present oscillations between listening with the third ear and not hearing what we listen to. I will consider such oscillations in terms of breakdown and restoration of empathic connection, and more generally the dynamic of destruction and survival, rupture, and repair. I draw on our increasing awareness of how analyst and patient together engage in dissociation in relation to troubling or terrifying feelings to show how the intersubjective third grows through reconnecting and surviving the mess those dissociations produce.

A crucial shift in clinical practice has evolved through our recognition of the power of dissociation, based on the "natural hypnoid capacity of mind," as Bromberg (2000) terms it. In particular, we have come to see that the analyst's involuntary response to the patient's dissociated self states is to dissociate herself. One might say that the very process of tracking so closely and becoming permeable to unconscious communication is what generates joint dissociation. Schore (2003), who has most comprehensively studied self- and mutual regulation in the therapy dyad, proposes that one partner's dissociation, which he sees as the movement from right to left hemisphere, is perceived and immediately produces a shift in the other. If, in response to the patient's hyperarousal, the analyst retreats from the "music" of mutual regulation (Knoblauch, 2000) into a dissociative use of observation in order to calm down, the patient can feel it.

In recent years the new emphasis on implicit relational knowing and empathic attunement helped correct for this dissociative use of observation so prevalent in the past. This shift in practice also implies, as relational analysts have emphasized (Bromberg, 1998; Davies, 2004) and I stress here, the awareness that the analyst's failures to attune and hurtful reopening of old wounds requires of her an internal struggle with self-regulation, her own shame and guilt—a struggle that takes place in the presence of someone who is listening to and monitoring the signs of her internal state.

After all, it is our goal for the patient to listen to himself as we listen, to understand himself as we understand ourselves (not just him). As analyst, in order to listen to the Other, I also have to be able to listen to myself, I have to be able to hear myself think, thinking about the other's message that is passing so rapidly through and inside me. If the other is hyperaroused, by shame or anxiety, I perhaps will be unable to hear myself think, the sound of that arousal will be too loud, the whoosh of the hormones in his blood stream and the alarm bells of his amygdala will ring in my ears. Perhaps it will be matched by my own internal voice, helpless about what to do next. Then again, before such anxiety can even take up full residence, the patient might move away from danger or I too, may cut off and resort to reassuringly distant thoughts, so that neither of us can hear what that stifled scream or tiny scared voice would be saying. Later, that shift will be registered—heard but not heard—by an off-note in the dialogues whose slight disjunctiveness attracts the notice of the supervisor (the observer in me or my colleague).

Invariably how I supervise when another clinician presents a case for consultation is to listen for that disjunctive moment; you might say I always look for the signs of dissociation, for the *not hearing*. From this blind spot the whole session or case may perhaps open up. My therapeutic approach begins with mindfulness of the process by which the patient and I together find a space, a rhythm of mutual accommodation, for me or us to hear what we are listening to. I presume that one of my primary tasks as analyst is to help the patient to help me in creating that space, for instance, by checking my response against his, sometimes aloud, sometimes mentally. Gradually, we will learn together to recover from ruptures in attunement, to become sensitive to the inexplicable gaps created by the patient's unintegrated, warring selves, or by waves of feeling that crash against unreceptive walls. These moments of excess that fail to evoke a mirroring knowledge, serve instead to signal the unformulated, undifferentiated malaise, despair or fear.

LISTENING AND THE INTERSUBJECTIVE PERSPECTIVE

This perspective on ruptures represents an amplification of my original effort to articulate the process of mutual recognition as one of breakdown and restoration of intersubjective space. Central to this viewpoint is a vision of clinical work as embedded in a flow between selves and listening as a shared process. For me the question of listening must therefore be posed in the context of an intersubjective perspective which takes account of reciprocal listening, of how the patient is registering and interpreting the analyst's experience, as relational authors such as Aaron (1996) and Hoffman (1983) have described.

Likewise essential to my view of intersubjectivity is the awareness that each partner in the therapeutic relation is registering the flow or dance they create together, which is governed by what may be called the third.

There are many ways of defining or describing the third. On one side, I find compelling and have often used the musical metaphor of how we create a third. It may be seen as a creation of a groove that may be broken and have to be re-created. But I am equally compelled by the metaphor of analysis as a theatre of enactment in which we are on the stage with the person we are listening to, participating in the drama with them such that it cannot be said who is scripting whom. Indeed, since we create this third together as we go along, it may be said to function as an improvisational script, as Ringstrom (2001, 2006) has elaborated. Each person follows and adds to that script, that third. The first, the musical metaphor, seems to capture the aspect of an interactive dance such as the one beginning with the mutual accommodation and co-created rhythm (Sander, 2002) in our earliest exchange of gestures with the mothering one. The second, the theatrical metaphor captures more of the narrative and symbolic elements of later interactions, though of course drama also includes the procedural level, the gestures, tone, and movement of the nonverbal. Both levels of the shared third encompass moments of listening and not listening, when the third breaks down and we struggle over who will write or direct it, whose version is right or wrong.

To be more precise, I have conceptualized the third not only in terms of the specific interactive pattern we follow as we create—an experience we might better call thirdness—but also the general principles of interaction that govern the process of co-creating recognition (Benjamin, 2004). These principles—often procedural rather than articulated—ground the experience of thirdness. Yet again, I think of the third as the process of realizing these principles in action: for instance, surviving breakdown with mutual recognition, moving from rupture to repair. In every dyad, we are not merely listening to or attuning to the other, but trying to follow the rhythm or music that accords with the third.

I have suggested (Benjamin, 2004) we use the term "primordial third," to designate the first, musical or rhythmic exchange of gestures between caretaker and child as well as the principle that underlies it—the procedural principles of lawful relating, involving accommodation, attunement and following expectable patterns (see Beebe and Lachmann, 1994; 2002). By contrast, the more developed "symbolic third," with its narrative elements, involves a more complex set of expectations, principles, and procedural rules that govern interactions based on consensus, negotiation, and recognition, especially recognition of the other's separate subjectivity.

Clearly empathy and attunement can be seen as elements of the primordial third, but they continue to find more developed expression in the symbolic third. In creating shared narratives about our experience, we strengthen the ability to balance mutual identification and difference, we evolve our capacity to differentiate or disagree while maintaining bonds of commonality. This is what I mean by recognition as a principle: we negotiate, play, clash, and reunite through the effort to meet the other's mind (Benjamin, 1995).

Because of the risks inherent in our "dangerous method," (Kerr, 1993) the inevitable failures of seeing and hearing that accompany this meeting of minds, it is necessary to introduce one more term. I use the term *moral third* to designate the essential principles—chief among them the valuing of truth, striving for accommodation, responsibility and respect for the other, and faith in the process of rupture and repair—that are common to both the primordial and the symbolic third (Benjamin, 2004; 2006). The moral third refers to those values, rules, and principles of interaction that we rely upon in our effort to create and restore the space for each partner in the dyad to engage in thinking, feeling, acting or responding rather than merely reacting.

In particular the principle of rupture and repair (Tronick, 2001) strikes me as essential; in therapeutic interaction the moral third is the principle to which we have recourse during impasse and lesser breakdowns. It is what we try to tune into when we find ourselves caught in the reciprocal lock of complementary relations (see Racker, 1968;

Benjamin, 1988) which characterize ruptures. In the split complementarity, which forms the structure of all breakdowns, a person is experienced as one's opposite pole, as in the relation of doer and done-to (Benjamin, 2004), accuser and accused, victimizer and victim, good and bad, right and wrong. Characteristically in such interactions there may be disagreement about who is the one doing to the other. At the same time, this is a dynamic in which neither person feels heard, neither can see the other's viewpoint, only one reality can prevail: yours or mine. The movement from the locked-in structure of complementarity with its see-saw polarities into the spacious opening of thirdness is something we subjectively experience as a liberation of our ability to feel and think. From the narrow space to freedom. It is often identified by its different capacity to hear multiple voices—I can hear both your voice and mine as can you; I can recognize what you felt, you can recognize what I felt. Or, the other's listening makes it possible for one of us to recognize the presence of multiple voices and parts of self.

The moral third becomes more urgently relevant as we increasingly accept the analyst's role in contributing to breakdown, rather than simply the one responsible for repairing it. This awareness of the analyst's contribution goes along with an examination of how the analyst may have dissociated along with the patient. This potential has led me to the paradox that analysts hurt as well as heal and therefore that patients—to reverse Winnicott's (1971) dictum—must become able to survive our destructiveness—or at the very least, our failures, lapses, dissociations, and vulnerabilities (Benjamin, 2006). The assumption that working through requires cycling together through loops of dissociations that include our participation as analyst leads to an emphasis on the moral third that requires the analyst to take responsibility for her failures. This principle underpins the perspective on the listening process that gives the utmost seriousness to developing a more careful listening to ourselves. But, I should add, this formulation is only useful to those who are willing to give up the ideal of being a "complete container," to surrender to the fact that we survive causing pain. When we think in terms of the third being renewed after breakdown or collapse it becomes possible to unite Winnicott's (1971) idea of one person surviving destruction with the principle of rupture and repair. My revision of Winnicott's idea highlights the need for reciprocal survival of failures in listening and communicating. In other words we truly accept that both partners—with their projective and dissociated processes—co-create a dialectic of breakdown and recognition. This is another take on the process of creating a stronger and more complex dyadic attachment system, which allows greater resilience in order to contain the deeply painful attachment histories of our patients as well as a transformative sense of mutual recognition.

A last theoretical point: The basic pattern of breakdown and repair of recognition can occur at either the procedural level of the primordial third or the symbolic third of negotiated understanding, or both. Difficulties arise, however, when repair is missing at the primordial level while the dynamic of rupture and repair appears to go on living at the symbolic level. That is why we have learned to listen more closely to signs of breakdown at the procedural level, the off-tones in the music of connection and attunement (Knoblauch, 2000), which signal dissociative gaps or the emergence of unknown, split off parts of self.

Each therapeutic dyad finds its way (or doesn't) to navigate the ebb and flow of dissociation and attunement, the breakdowns in shared thirdness. Empathy and attunement are book-ended by enactment and breakdown into complementarity on one side, by detachment, boredom, and what we might call *in-actment* on the other. By in-actment I mean those enactments that are stillborn, because their content is hidden by inaction, deliberate avoidance of the clash or rupture. We might imagine charting the basic rhythm (Eigen, 2005) of rupture and restoration, of finding our way back into attunement, as a wave, or many waves, with varying duration from seconds to minutes to weeks or months. But if the wave of symbolic understanding follows a different line on the graph than the affective experiencing of that wave, the two levels of the third may be unlinked. Indeed, they often are initially unlinked when we first move into areas of trauma or pain. Therefore the failure to hear both simultaneously, to find ourselves unable to link states and feelings that are indeed generating anxiety and hence dissociative reactions, should be recognized as a liability intrinsic to our work and not really as a failure at all. By the same token, it is in the nature of our work to become detached from and unable to listen to our multiple inner voices as well. One voice drowns out the other—perhaps forcing each partner to speak only the opposite of the other or leaving one part of the patient feeling unheard.

THE CLINICAL SITUATION

The disconnect between levels of experience, the moving out of deep listening, the tuning out, and other forms of in-actment, were rife in the psychoanalytic field during the time in which interpretation was viewed as a summum bonum, the telos of our work. One of the most common transitions from in-actment to enactment would then result from what used to be called bad timing in interpretation. Generally, this consisted of the analyst reaching for the symbolic third in his own mind and so inadvertently revealing to the patient that he was indeed conversing with, listening to, someone else—that is, himself (see Britton, 1988). While the "good patient" could benefit from listening in to the analyst's conversation, the "bad patient" (that is, the non-speaking part of the same person) felt shut out and not listened to.

This sort of event led the neo-Kleinians to formulate the idea of the patient feeling excluded from the third, which was understood as a form of primal coupling with theory in the analyst's own mind. Whereas Feldman (1993) saw the patient's dislike of this as a reaction against unwelcome proof that the analyst can have his own thoughts just as mother could have father and leave him out, Britton (1988) seemed rather more sympathetic to the sense in which the patient's sense of being left out, abandoned, was a reaction to feeling uncontained by the analyst. For those with an already shaky maternal container, Britton realized, such side conversations between mother and father would constitute misattunement, regardless of its apparent accuracy. Elaborating this idea further (Aaron and Benjamin, 1999), a relational analyst might want to recognize this internal conversation as disruptive to the shared conversation—the third—and especially to identifying with and engaging the voice that the patient is having trouble expressing at the moment. It might, for instance, constitute an exclusive conversation with the "good" part of the patient. Usually, when the analyst takes refuge in a detached observing third bolstered by "accurate" insight into the patient he is already feeling unable to speak in a way that the patient could hear. He is thus already involved in a dissociative move that mirrors or further activates the patient's move away from the feared part of herself. Such moves can be felt painfully, despairingly by the patient even when she has moved away first or when she recognizes the analyst's insight as having validity.

After all, the patient's conviction that the analyst doesn't want to know her dissociated self state is part of why she isn't able to put it out directly to begin with. Her belief that there is no one willing to witness the pain and despair of that self is a major constituent of the interactive dynamic (Slavin, cited in Benjamin, 2006). The pair have yet to construct a witnessing place for the analyst in relation to that part of the patient. My basic thesis is that just as the third must be co-created by the analytic couple, with the facilitating knowledge of the analyst aiming in that direction, so the place for the analyst as adequate listener and witness, specific to the multiple parts of this patient, is created by the partners together.

To create a symbolic third that allows the conflicting feelings of different self-parts to be known requires a conversation between the right witness and the "right" part—ultimately many parts—of the patient. The thing the patient is simultaneously trying to prevent being known and get the analyst to know through enactment—the thing he wants and doesn't want her to hear—has to become manifest in the presence of a witness. Yet the witness in this case is already suspect of being an unwilling bystander, if not an outright injurer, so that the analyst must survive her own disregulation of feeling shame and guilt about being absent or off-base—often, and she must do this while trying to contain the shame-based rage that the patient feels at being unheard.

Ted Jacobs has generously provided us with some beautiful clinical analysis which ably dissects this kind of enactment, in which the analyst becomes a usable listener in his article "On Misreading and Misleading Patients" (2001). In the case of Ms. N., Jacobs finds himself bored and distracted, unable to listen, fingering a spiral notebook as the patient speaks from a place of avoiding pain and, in particular, the recently mentioned sexual molestation by her cousin. As the patient remarks that she feels him to be uninterested, distracted, and perhaps stroking something, Jacobs takes the opportunity to interpret that these stroking sounds are familiar to her. Ms. N. gets it, takes up the link to her cousin, admits that she is scared of lying down, even adds some derogatory comments about not putting it past male analysts to make use of the situation to exploit the patient. She also admits that she feels crazy because she imagines that Jacobs really is like her father. Now Jacobs must deal with knowing that he actually had tuned out the patient and that, because of his shame and guilt, had used interpretation to mislead her rather than acknowledging the truth of her perceptions.

But it was through this misleading, not just tuning out and fiddling with his notebook, that the enactment could be fully staged. Jacob's use of the analytic posture to sidestep the patient's accurate perception, this dissociative handling of his own reactions is what constituted crucial elements of the replay of the past, which included the cousin's denial and demand for secrecy. Only by tuning her out—as he termed it—did he fully tune in to her and the thing she was tuning out. In this way the full drama presented itself on the stage, the purloined letter was placed in plain view. Crucial to Jacob's work with the patient was that he determined to focus her attention on the enactment and acknowledge his part in it.

Jacobs offers a useful explanation for the need to acknowledge, for otherwise such misleading interpretation puts the patient in an impossible bind. I would say, the patient was accurately listening in on the analyst's mind but believed she had to protect him, because he was too weak to survive the knowledge that she could hear his guilt and shame over not being present. The acknowledgment made it clear that he could survive her knowing him and his difficulty. First, however, their initial collusion allowed them to re-enact the shame and guilt both of the molester and the one being molested, the kind of locked-in complementarity that we see in enactments. The enactment allowed the dissociated experience to emerge, and the rupture gave the opportunity for a deeper level of recognition and repair through acknowledgment. I would argue that this only works because, as Jacobs showed, the analyst survived the confrontation by acknowledging his actions, which also freed him to analyze himself truthfully. Now more voices could be heard, each partner having survived: The analyst survived the patient's attack, the patient the analyst's absence and misleading. The shared third was strengthened, and with it the moral third supporting the analyst as listener who can provide acknowledgment and facilitate mutual understanding.

The acknowledgment of having abandoned the patient is crucial in view of another dissociation that interfered with listening. Ms. N. presumably had deep doubt about the analyst's willingness to listen to the voice of pain and shame, to witness her suffering. Her desperate, unmet need for such recognition was, however, dissociated from the telling of the story about her cousin, and so was followed by withdrawal and boredom. The despairing needy self, presumably originating in her basic attachment history, was expressed in her desire for her cousin's valuable attention, and yet that need was actually dissociated in the sexual molestation. The despairing needy self might also be said to motivate the analytic enactment of the dyad "abandoned child/neglectful parent," who refuses to know or witness. In such enactments, we have greater difficulty addressing the abandonment because we as analysts are now enacting it, must listen to the other's pain when we ourselves have caused it. However when, as Ferenczi (1933) originally advised, we acknowledge our repetition of the injury we are in effect inviting the abandoned part to become more vocal. We thus avoid repeating the part where the original abuser or bystander adult denied the child's reality. In my view, what produces retraumatization is not the enactment itself but the lack of working through, including especially an analyst's failure to acknowledge, which the patient correctly grasps as the *avoidable* failure. I want to further illustrate these themes of abandonment, dissociation, and acknowledgment with a patient who put me in mind of Jacob's case of Ms. N.

A DETAILED ILLUSTRATION

My patient Hannah, now approaching the end of a long analysis, lay weary on the couch not even wanting to talk about the dream she'd had for the umpteenth time about not fitting in at work, being inferior to her male colleagues and less glamorous than the female ones. Maybe it would be better to talk about some recent occurrences with her child, this stuff about being less successful and not fitting in was getting so boring, she said. After doing just that Hannah paused and began describing a strange reaction she'd had after watching the film *To Die For*, in which the glamorous, murderous Nicole Kidman exploits, among others, the pathetic overweight teenage girl sidekick who adulates her. This is a girl who has been molested and forever neglected, who's never had anyone give her attention or encouragement. Hannah tells me that while she had laughed raucously at Kidman during the film, she found herself feeling weirder and weirder afterward, almost disoriented. I took her statement about feeling weird to indicate that some dissociated, unformulated feelings were pressing to be known, and asked her if she could tell me more. She was then able to focus her attention on the girl, realizing that of course she must identify with her—Hannah herself having been seduced as a fourteen-year-old by a friend of her father's and been sexually acting out since the age of twelve.

Despite having talked about this horribly shameful adolescence, this period has remained the dark side of the moon for an analysis that appeared to have gone rather well, given the extraordinary changes in the patient's life, the success she actually has achieved, the attractive appearance she now does project, her gratification in marriage and children. At the same time, that intractable complaint of inferiority and failure remained unresolved, a legacy of a part of self resented and ineffectually hidden. In fact this hated girl had been railed against in countless sessions from the beginning of treatment. The opening to this particularly shameful self that was afraid to be found yet clamoring to be heard was blocked by self-beratement which early in the analysis I had often found it quite difficult to listen to. With time we were able to create enough calm to parse out her identification with the "one who was doing the beating" as Guntrip's patient famously put it, and we had come to repeat her quip about her self-beating, transforming Flaubert's "Emma, c'est moi!" into "Hitler c'est moi." Naming the expectation that I would join the one doing the beating and decoding her once abundant masochistic fantasies and dreams was a constant part of our dialogue, but not always noticeably transformative.

For in spite of that naming, that expectation had to be enacted. Moments inevitably arose when Hannah felt me to be the persecuting complement to her victimhood, while I felt as if forced to be a helpless witness to her attacks on her shameful, "monstrous" self. But in a rapid reversal of the complementarily, I as bystander could cause her pain by seeing her too positively, by failing to grasp how desperate her plight was, as she imagined herself about to lose her job, be disgraced forever. To be empathetic was to be one with her despair; to think she had not ruined herself socially and professionally forever was to be in denial of her dissociated but powerful sense of catastrophe, which was overlayed by such deep shame. As long as the wound whose opening would bring that catastrophe remained hidden, it seemed as if we were caught in an unending choice between false reassurance or despair. My resistance to being forced to hear a pain I could not relieve functioned as an analogue to her feeling of submission to persecution. In this complementary breakdown my failure matched hers.

Hannah's mother had always responded to her accounts of being excluded in childhood with anxious despair—the opposite of the soothing mother who can hear her baby's pain and mark her expression (Fonagy et al., 2002) to show that she understands the baby's distress but is not one with it. Herself constantly disregulated and hyperaroused, this mother lacked all belief in her ability to soothe and create a rhythmic third with her baby. Thus in the enactments created by self-attacks I had to struggle to maintain contact with Hannah's need for a soothing mother and to regulate my sense of inadequacy about not being able to console or soothe her. The more Hannah needed soothing, the more she felt a traumatic certainty that the Other would fail her, that she was unworthy.

A turning point came when she returned from a weekend with some other young people with a familiar tale of woe. Unable to engage in witty banter, she became withdrawn, excruciatingly uncomfortable, as she felt observed scornfully by her friends. In this instance I did not question her extravagant conviction of failure but spoke as if it were true, directly from a protective indignation. I allowed myself to feel as if she really were my own child whom I considered at least a match for her friends in integrity, personal insight and intelligence. But I also spoke from a connection to a particular moral third. I asked her why she thought her anxiety and vulnerability were so unacceptable and why she didn't deserve understanding and compassion from her friends, which she would surely have given had the situation been reversed. To my surprise, Hannah began the next session with an unusual response, saying how surprised and gratified she was by my "staunch defense." What she was able to hear this time was not a refusal to bear her despair or witness her demise, but rather my presence at her side defending a way of connecting, a principle. She allowed as how she had thought she was facing reality, trying to take responsibility for her problems by identifying with her friend's judgment of her but it suddenly occurred to her that there was a different way to listen. I suggested that she indeed did identify with this kind of judgment, in fact, she probably elicited their contempt because she shared it. She agreed, "Yes, I do Shtick, I make a Shtick out of vulnerability when I'm anxious." I said, yes, it really is a Stick—you punish yourself with it, and invite people to join you. What you have to be responsible for is not your vulnerability but your punishing and beating yourself, for your lack of compassion toward you."

What fostered our move into cooperative narrative reconstruction of the drama, a shared symbolic third, including insight without shame into her preference to hurt herself before the other could hurt her? The music of my indigant defense? My introducing the idea of a witness or listener who feels compassion? Certainly, Hannah heard my true subjective response, my indignation as a protest—"Stop beating her!"—which her mother was not strong enough to make, for instance against her father's contempt. What she identified with was a moral third, a vision of strength—my own—that came not from hating the shame-filled parts of self, but accepting psychic pain. This moral third makes it possible both to accord safety and respect to the fragile, frightened part of her and hold in mind her strength, not least her dignity as a person struggling to understand her own pain and that of others. It allowed both selves to be present at the same time.

Quite a bit later she reflected on just how much my willingness to enact the role of a protective mother who stands up for her child played a part. It was this improvisational role that enabled a shift away from submission, her clinging to a look-alike imitation of the observing third—"I know I am responsible." Embracing this simulacrum of insight that embodied her punitive self-scrutiny represented her effort to appear normal, acceptable, lovable. Letting go of this appearance, she was able to move into the thirdness based on an idea of compassionate witnessing that comes from a place of respect for human vulnerability. She said that what I had given her was a moral universe, in which she had learned about compassion. It was, I believe, this shift toward compassionate listening that allowed her soon thereafter to start up the relationship with the man she married. And, immediately after the session I described, she was able to tell me for the first time about the desperately promiscuous adolescent girl, to admit her humiliation and loneliness.

In this year's reprise, when the dissociative moment after the movie raises a curtain again on her monster teenage self, it finally becomes linked to the same character as the self doomed to fail in her daily life as an adult. The relationship to Nicole helps to link young Hannah's

to create mutual containment. Thus, Hannah was ready to jump at the chance to maintain my image as a complete container out of a need to preserve a usable ideal, and her fear that otherwise all ideal properties would be destroyed. Together we had to create a framework in which the idealized field of witnessing and listening included rupture and failure. We had to replace the ideals of invulnerability and complete containing, to which she had aspired at such a high price, to defend against shameful need of the other.

The alternative to the ideal of the analyst as complete container is the relational view that the analyst "has to change" (Slavin and Kriegman, 1998). The analyst exemplifies the patient's internal struggle (Mitchell, 1997) and models the process of transcending failure, having faith that through rupture and repair, losing and refinding the rhythm of recognition, analyst and patient survive together and build a stronger third. In this view the patient learns by watching the analyst struggle to hear different voices, to listen to herself and confront what she hears and not only to the patient.

Here is what one patient wrote about watching the analyst embody her own struggles. This was a woman physically abused in childhood, who had threatened my life shortly after dreams brought forth her own terror of being killed by her parents and of being flayed alive by her therapist. This patient felt terrified that neither of us would survive the other's violence, she could not imagine any moral third that would protect her. She articulated in the most forceful way how she needed to know that I was acting out of my own personal faith that wounds could be healed and violence overcome, not out of professional design and distance. In her therapeutic diary that she shared with me in each session, written in a calm after these extremely violent terrors and impulses emerged, she wrote: "J thinks that I like to keep her uninformed, in the dark, stumbling amidst obstacles...I'm just so amazed that she eventually finds he way back on course, that she recognizes wrong turns and misinterpretaions, has the courage, authenticity and confidence to acknowledge it, that she has the fortitude to continue...and that in spite of this being an unreal relationship, she is insistently real.....It doesn't give me pleasure to see her groping, but it's so fascinating to watch. Besides the fact that I think wrong turns are a source of many discoveries, J is not idealized at all when she's stumbling. And since idealization is the major obstacle in my life—at the same time that it's utterly life-giving—how I idealize her (keep her unreal) or realize her (keep her un-ideal)—is very important."

The ideal so long embraced by analysts of the analyst-listener as a "complete container" was precisely the one this patient had to rupture in order to touch something solid and believable. In many cases the attempt to live up to that ideal left the analyst no option but to deal with enactment by mystifying the patient in order to protect the analyst. In the process, the analyst dissociated from the extreme danger in which the patient found herself, having to either forfeit her sense of reality or her connection to the analyst.

Yet, having recognized this dilemma, we have nonetheless plenty of experience with more severely traumatized patients for whom it is no light matter for the analyst to shoulder responsibility for participating in the enactment. When such serious trauma is re-enacted the patient's felt sense of danger erases the distinction between the analyst dissociating the patient's pain and terror, that is, the failure in witnessing, and the analyst actually perpetrating the crime. When the analyst tries to bear responsibility for the injury that is being re-enacted, it can appear both as an intolerable threat to the patient's safety as well as to one's identity as a reliable healer. Thus we can all recognize the felt danger both analyst and patient may experience in the face of the analyst's dissociative missteps. Yet, as the patient I just quoted showed, it is also possible to make enough of one's own process observable that the patient can watch and listen without feeling she has to deny and protect the caregiver lest she be forever cast out or guilty of destroying her, when she can enjoy watching the analyst grope, listening to her as an other whom she both idealizes and de-idealizes, a new field of mutual listening is created.

I am clarifying that expecting the patient to contain or survive some knowledge of our failures, is not asking him to hold the hot potato, absorb all the badness in the relationship. It is not tantamount to expecting forgiveness—further excoriation might be the patient's best immediate response, as we saw with Jacob's patient. On the contrary, it demonstrates a sense of solidity that can tolerate scrutiny by the other. A certain form of acknowledgment transforms the complementary see-saw of blame and invites the patient to be an interpreter, a listener as well as a speaker. To help create a shared third, take account of what each one has been hearing, how each has been listening to what is happening. It is an action that develops faith in the *moral third* because it affirms the lawful ethic of responsibility and counteracts past experiences of denial. Such action is meant to show that the analyst *can* change, and that revealing her struggle to do so transforms the analytic process into one of mutual listening to multiple voices.

REFERENCES

Aaron, L. 1995. The internalized primal scene. *Psychoanalytic Dialogues* 5: 195–237.

———. 1996. *A Meeting of Minds: Mutuality in Psychoanalysis*. Hillsdale, NJ: Analytic Press.

———. 1999. Clinical choices and the relational matrix. *Psychoanalytic Dialogues* 9: 1–30.

Aaron, L. and J. Benjamin. 1999. Intersubjectivity and the struggle to think. Paper presented at Spring Meeting, Division 39 of the American Psychological Association, New York, April.

Beebe, B. and F. Lachmann. 1994. Representation and internalization in infancy: three principles of salience. *Psychoanalytic Psychology* 11: 127–165.

———. 2002. *Infancy Research and Adult Treatment*. Hillsdale, NJ: Analytic Press.

Benjamin, J. 1988. *The Bonds of Love: Psychoanalysis, Feminism, and the Problem of Domination*. New York: Pantheon.

———. 1995. Recognition and destruction: an outline of intersubjectivity. In: *Like Subjects, Love Objects*. New Haven, CT: Yale University Press.

———. 2004. Beyond doer and done-to: an intersubjective view of thirdness. *Psychoanalytic Quarterly* 73: 5–46.

———. 2006. Our appointment in Thebes: acknowledging the analyst's fear of doing harm. Paper presented at the International Association for Relational Psychoanalysis and Psychotherapy, Boston, January 30, 2006.

Britton, R. 1988. The missing link: parental sexuality in the Oedipus complex. In: *The Contemporary Kleinians of London*, ed. R. Shafer, pp. 242–258. Madison, CT: International Universities Press, 1997.

Bromberg, P. 1998. Staying the same while changing: reflections on clinical judgment. *Psychoanalytic Dialogue* 8: 225–236.

———. 2000. Potholes on the royal road—or is it an abyss. *Contemporary Psychoanalysis* 36: 5–28.

Davies, J. 2004. Whose bad objects are we anyway?: repetition and our elusive love affair with evil. *Psychoanalytic Dialogues* 14: 711–732.

Davies, J. and M. Frawley. 1994. *Treating the Adult Survivor of Childhood Sexual Abuse: A Psychoanalytic Perspective*. New York: Basic Books.

Eigen, M. 2005. *The Sensitive Self.* Middletown, CT: Wesleyan University Press.

Feldman, M. 1993. The dynamics of reassurance. In: *The Contemporary Kleinians of London*, ed. R. Shafer, pp. 321–344. Madison, CT: International Universities Press, 1997.

Ferenczi, S. 1933. The confusion of tongues between adult and child. Reprinted, *Contemporary Psychoanalysis*, 1990.

Fonagy, P., G. Gergely, E. Jurist, and M. Target. 2002. *Affect Regulation, Mentalization and the Development of the Self.* New York/London: Other Books.

Hoffman, I.Z. 1983. The patient as interpreter of the analyst's experience. *Contemporary Psychoanalysis* 19: 389–422.

Jacobs, T. 2001. On misreading and misleading patients: some reflections on communications, miscommunications, and countertransference enactments. *International Journal of Psychoanalysis* 82: 653–670.

Kerr, J. 1993. *A Most Dangerous Method: The Story of Jung, Freud, and Sabina Spielrein*. New York: Knopf.

Knoblauch, S. H. 2000. *The Musical Edge of Therapeutic Dialogue*. Hillsdale, NJ: Analytic Press.

Lacan, J. 1975. *The Seminar of Jacques Lacan, Book I, 1953–1954*, trans. J. Forrester. New York: Norton, 1991.

———. 1977. *Ecrits*, trans. A.Sheridan. New York: Norton.

Mitchell, S. 1997. *Influence and Autonomy in Psychoanalysis*. Hillsdale, NJ: Analytic Press.

Racker, H. 1968. *Transference and Countertransference*. London: Karnac, 1982.

Ringstrom, P. 2001. Cultivating the improvisational in psychoanalytic treatment. *Psychoanalytic Dialogue* 11: 727–754.

———. 2006. Scenes that write themselves: improvisational moments in relational psychoanalysis. *Psychoanalytic Dialogues* 16: in press.

Sander, L. 2002. Thinking differently: principles of process in living systems and the specificity of being known. *Psychoanalytic Dialogues* 12: 11–42.

Schore, A. N. 2003. *Affect Regulation and the Repair of the Self.* New York: Norton.

Slavin, M. and D. Kriegman. 1998. Why the analyst needs to change. *Psychoanalytic Dialogues* 8: 247–285.

Tronick, E. Z. 2001. Emotional connection and dyadic consciousness in infant-mother and patient-therapist interactions. *Psychoanalytic Dialogues* 11: 187–194.

Winnicott, D. W. 1971. The use of an object and relating through identifications. In: *Playing and Reality*. London: Tavistock.

5

LISTENING TO THE CHILD WITHIN

Discussion of Benjamin's Chapter "Listening Together: Intersubjective Aspects of the Analytic Process of Losing and Restoring Recognition"

Theodore Fallon, M.D.

In 1816, a French physician named Laennec devised a way of listening to the heart with the assistance of an invention called the stethoscope. Laennec heard and described the familiar 'lub-dub' sounds. Thereafter, tens of thousands of practitioners from around the world listened to millions of patients and heard the same familiar 'lub-dub.' Then in 1968 after 162 years of listening, someone heard a new sound that no one had heard before, the S4. Can you imagine the excitement of the moment:

> "Listen! I hear another sound just before the 'lub.' "
> "No. This is no other sound."
> "Yes. There it is. Listen."
> "I don't hear it."

That is the experience I had in reading Dr. Jessica Benjamin's paper. The excitement of hearing something that has not been heard even with a century of listening. To hear a new sound, one has to listen in a new way. But how do you explain about listening in a new way when there is only the old available with which to begin. It is a major feat to write such a paper. I see Dr. Benjamin as having done this. It is also a feat to make this discovery for oneself as every reader and listener must do for themselves. Dr. Benjamin invites us to do that with her.

The recursive nature of listening to a paper about listening provides an opportunity to study the process even as we are doing it. For me, reading this paper was an opportunity to meet a strange new other with a language unfamiliar to me. I initially experienced a rupture in my relationship with the other, in this case the writer. This was, of course, due to my ignorance. I persisted and found a tutor in intersubjectivity speak, Barbara Goldsmith. As a new awareness began to creep in, there was a restoration of meaning, a repair, and I was deeply enriched by the experience of understanding this paper. Dr. Benjamin describes all of this in her paper.

Let me here restate the concept of intersubjectivity as I understand it. Two parties enter into a process of psychotherapy/psychoanalysis and create a shared reality between them. Dr. Benjamin calls this shared reality the 'third.' This 'third' might be likened to Winnicott's transitional phenomenon (Winnicott, 1953, p. 18). The difference is that Dr. Benjamin's space ('the third') is shared by the two parties who are co-creating the space. When all is going well, there is a synchrony. Each party in the synchrony freely contributes to this 'third' space by bringing forward and sharing parts of themselves. The problem occurs when one of the parties does not want to know about a particular part of him/herself, but this self continues to seek expression (also known as return of the repressed). This unknown part of the self of the first party is dissociated and generates dissociation in the second party. One might translate this process as projective identification where one person gets another involved in an enactment. When there is no external action, but rather avoiding of an action, as occurs in dissociation, Dr. Benjamin calls this 'inactment' (Benjamin, 2007, p. 19). Dr. Benjamin is careful here, however, to avoid putting the responsibility of the process on any one of the parties. Both parties are responsible for creating 'the third.'

Dr. Benjamin carefully examines the enactment using the terms 'complementarity,' 'mutual regulation' and 'dysregulation of shame,' 'the rupture of the relationship,' "collapse of the 'third'." In this context, she offers a process to help reconstruct the 'third' where both parties can again contribute. This reconstruction process is where I heard the new heart sound. In an enactment (or 'inactment'), how does the therapist fully take responsibility for his part, even if he was unknowingly led in to participating?

And how can the therapist reinforce a sense of respect for all of the selves in the patient, even when one of the selves that sought but was denied expression, misled the therapist? Dr. Benjamin suggests that rather than attempting to humble the patient into submission with an interpretation, the therapist admits his misstep thereby verifying the patient's perception. In this admission, the therapist is calling the patient's attention to the patient's own dissociation, inviting that dissociated part of the patient's self into the 'third,' paving the way for the repair of the relationship and resumption of the third now with more of the patient involved and invested.

Dr. Benjamin's paper deals with this interaction as it relates to adult patients, but she does not describe how this process goes with children in therapy. Nor does she put this process into a developmental context although her work is clearly derived from early mother/infant observations. In my discussion, I would like to provide some reflections on this intersubjective process of listening as it relates to children and development.

To do this, I wish to use some well-examined concepts. For the sake of brevity, I will refer to these concepts in the literature but will not fully explicate them here. The concepts include theory of mind (Bretherton and Beeghly, 1982), development of mentalization (Fonagy and Target, 1998), projective identification as explained by Klein's (1935, 1946) paranoid position and its resolution by a movement toward the depressive position (1940), Winnicott's (1960) view of development as an interaction between mother and child, and the more recent empirical observations and explanations of early child development as a co-creation by mother and child (Stern, 1985).

An exciting aspect of Dr. Benjamin's work for me is that this new way of listening can be understood and further explicated by these developmental concepts and observations, and through this exploration offers the possibility of enriching child and adult psychoanalytic practice and theory.

DEVELOPMENT OF THE CORE SELF

The starting point of this exploration will be the concept of projective identification that was mentioned earlier in relation to the enactment/inactment process that Dr. Benjamin described. In her paper, Dr. Benjamin avoids referring to projective identification. She may do this because most people would associate this term with placing the responsibility of enactment at the patient's feet. Klein (1946), however, and for that matter Winnicott (1949), referred to a process like projective identification that occurs normally in development. This concept comes into play for Klein in the paranoid position that she describes, which also embodies a concept that Dr. Benjamin refers to as 'complementarity' (see also Seligman, 1999).

For Winnicott, a process like projective identification begins at birth when the infant looks for and finds an image of himself in the eye of the mother. For example, the infant cries but only knows discomfort. Mother anticipates the child's need to feed and feeds the infant. Through repeated experience of this mother-child event, the child learns about his experience of hunger and the need for food. Fonagy and Target (1996) refer to this process as the essence of what builds the core of the self early in development. When the parent adequately reflects back to the child the child's as yet unknown experience of himself, a healthy core self develops.

The reflection that the parent provides must be close enough to the infant's experience so that the infant can recognize it, but it must also be developmentally appropriate. The infant cannot take on the full burden of reality (e.g., "You infant suffer from a very mild hunger which pains you deeply, but it could get a lot worse. You are also helpless to obtain food for yourself. Food is obtained by fitting into society, acquiring skills and a job, making money so you can buy the food and delaying all sorts of other gratifications in this planning process").

It is also not appropriate for the parent to convey the interpersonal implications—"You know, I have to get up in the middle of my sleep which is inconvenient as I have all sorts of other responsibilities let alone desires—so I can feed you." Of course, this is not appropriate for the infant. All of this, however, is appropriate for later in the child's development. It is with the developmentally appropriate picture of the child in mind that the good, responsible, and loving parent approaches the child. If we look at that picture of the child, it is a picture that is accurate enough for the child, with their limited understanding and knowledge, to recognize themselves and their own experience.

As a side note, for practical purposes, the parent cannot reflect back to the child a picture that is entirely consonant with the one that the child has of himself and his experience. But for theoretical purposes, if this picture could be perfect—that is, if the parent perfectly anticipated and perfectly addressed every experience of the child, there would be no push for the child to grow. There is an optimal level of frustration that promotes growth. Too much or too little frustration interferes with growth. This concept can be demonstrated using pure tones. If the child emits a tone and the parent perfectly reflects that tone, it sounds as one. In this case, the child would only experience a magnification of his own internal experience. If the parent's reflection is just slightly off, the child can hear himself as well as the parent and can compare the two. In this way, the child is gratified and also has an opportunity to experience evidence of the outside world. If however, the parent's tone is too much different than the child's tone, the dissonance becomes painful. The child experiences frustration in not feeling joined with himself or with another. This frustrating situation may generate hostility (Parens, 1991).

For Dr. Benjamin, too, the slightly-off tone of the patient that the therapist reflects back to the patient are not just impossible to avoid, but seems to be necessary. The developmental model of how a core self is formed would suggest that there is an optimal level of frustration in which the therapist reflects back a good enough picture of the patient's experience. That experience of course would include the patient's perception of the therapist who has a significant role in the patient's development as the parent does in the child's life.

The developmental model further points out that although the developing child has his own contributions and independent perceptions, the relationship between the parent and child is asymmetric. The parent has certain powers (though not all powerful), burdens, and responsibilities above and beyond what the developing child has. I believe this asymmetry is implied in Dr. Benjamin's model in the extra burden that the therapist bears in being sensitive to, conscious of, and responsible for clarifying the interaction. I believe there are also certain *powers* of which the therapist has that he must assiduously be aware, including the power to excite the libido.

When a good parent approaches a child, it is with the child's experiences and abilities in mind—in other words, with his development in mind. Although there is considerable variation from child to child, normative development offers expectations of the child's capabilities and as yet undeveloped aspects, and informs a parent of the asymmetry that has to be accounted for in any interaction. When all goes well in child development, the parent adequately reflects back to the child the child's experience of himself and the world, and the child develops a healthy core self.

If we understand psychoanalysis as assisting development, then the therapist's reflecting back to the patient his experiences is a similar process. Then what Dr. Benjamin is describing can be understood as promoting repair or healthy development of a core self in the patient. The challenge for a therapist in working with adults, however, is that the level of development is potentially extremely variable, even within the same patient, depending on the degree of regression and level of functioning. In that case, the extent of the asymmetry between patient and therapist is much more difficult to anticipate.

THE PSYCHIC EQUIVALENT AND THE PRETEND MODES OF THINKING

Once a healthy core self has been established, the child's mind seems to be able to operate in one of two modes: the "psychic equivalent mode" and the "pretend mode" (Fonagy and Target, 1996). These modes tend to operate exclusive of one another and initially may not safely operate together. In the "psychic equivalent mode," the child has an image of the outside world in his mind. The child understands this image not as an idea but as a replica of the world. That is, the child has no awareness of thoughts as separate from reality. He has no concept of a mind thinking thoughts—neither in his own mind nor in that of another. I am referring here to the concept of 'theory of mind.'

An example is provided by Ashington and Gopnick (1988). The child at three years of age is shown a box with a picture of chocolates on the outside and asked what he thinks is in the box. The child replies, "chocolates." He is then shown the contents of the box, pencils. He is then asked what he thought was in the box when he first saw the box. The child replies, "pencils."

The child at age three is unable to conceptualize the difference between his thoughts and reality. What is outside the mind is the same as what is inside. There are many clinical examples in the literature about how thoughts on the inside bring about changes in perception of the external world. Of course this world of psychic equivalent is terrifying when one has angry, or even murderous thoughts and cannot see the difference between thoughts and their execution. The child has no control over the world anymore than he would have control over his thoughts. In fact, the psychic equivalent mode of thinking is what gives psychosis its power.

The second mode of thinking at this stage of development is the "pretend mode" (Fonagy and Target, 1996). In this mode, the child is able to manipulate thoughts in a kind of symbolic processing, but these symbols have no relation to the outside world in the child's mind. For example, we can see a child at three years of age play creatively. The child, however, will not consider the relationship between the elements of his play and the outside world, although the relationships may be obvious to an adult who is watching. If attempts are made to force the child to consider the relationship between his play and the outside world, his play may be disrupted (Erikson, 1940).

MENTALIZATION

When a parent (or a trusted other) mediates between these two modes of thinking—the pretend mode and the psychic equivalent mode—progressive development for the child is supported. This happens in play therapy and also happens between a parent and child in normal development. The other provides a safe place where the child can find his ideas and feelings in pretend mode. The child projects these thoughts on to the other who processes them and reflects them back to the child. The reflections back need to be safe and reasonably accurate to match the child's perceptions so the child can recognize them.

Through this interpersonal (intersubjective) process, the child builds a repertoire of safe connections between pretend mode and psychic equivalent mode. In the normal course of development when the thoughts reflected back to the child provide an optimal balance between harmony and dissonance, the child is provided an opportunity to recognize his own thoughts as different from but related to the outside world. With repeated experiences, the child begins to realize that his thoughts are safe to reflect on. This process of self-reflection is what Fonagy refers to as mentalization.

This self-reflection evolves in what the child perceives as his 'private transitional space.' However, its development is facilitated by another through play. The child's attachment to and trust of the other is critical in this process. Therefore, the child's ability to reflect on the outside world is dependent on and facilitated by the child's attachment to the other. In this sequence, we can see that intersubjective interpersonal attachment to another leads cognition. And, from the other's perspective, what goes on the child's 'private transitional space' is created by contributions from both the child and the other in the context of a relationship.

From the perspective of the child, we see Winnicott's (1953) transitional phenomenon, but from the other's perspective, we see Benjamin's 'third' that the child does not yet recognize for developmental reasons. It is only with the development of mentalization that the child recognizes that this transitional space is co-created with another. And within this transitional space, the child can recognize his own thoughts and thoughts of another, and can see them as separate, although related to the outside world.

Considering this same function of self-reflection from a Kleinian perspective, the infant moves from the paranoid position where there is no room for another (me versus the world) to the depressive position where there is now room for another. In this process, the child relinquishes control of the other and must mourn the loss of this control over the other, but also gains the ability to co-create with another. At the same time, he moves from the psychic equivalent/pretend mode dichotomy to a more integrated form of thinking that allows him to be aware of and think about thoughts, his and another's.

This process can be seen in therapy with adults. In fact Klauber (1987) describes psychoanalysis as a pretend experience although I would add that in the cases that Dr. Benjamin describes, the psychic equivalent/pretend mode dichotomy is in operation around the key issues. For these cases, both modes operating together have been unsafe. As a clinician, Dr. Benjamin is careful in attempting to create a safe setting within the therapeutic 'transitional space.' When an attempt fails, as it has failed for the patient many times before, Dr. Benjamin is careful to reflect back to the patient his experience, creating a safe connection between the psychic equivalent and the pretend mode. Respect for all of the patient's selves is critical in creating this safe setting. This process assists adults toward the development of self-reflection in those areas where they have had difficulty with their self-reflection. In Dr. Benjamin's terms, there is an "opening of the third."

A CLINICAL ILLUSTRATION

I will now provide a fragment from a case of a child to demonstrate these developmental concepts in clinical work with children. D was a very bright and engaging eight-year-old girl who had repeatedly accused her mother of child abuse. In the one event that I was able to observe, after D repeatedly provoked her mother over a period of days, D made the mother late for an important appointment by very slowly getting ready for school. In her frustration, the mother tossed a paperback book toward the child, hitting the child on the forehead. With a bruise now on her forehead, D was taken to school by mother. When D arrived, she went to a guidance counselor and complained that her mother had attempted to beat her this morning and she had escaped this beating by running away and now had no where to go. The counselor called child protective services who immediately placed the child in an emergency foster home. Within a week after this incident, D was returned home, the abuse charge determined to be unfounded.

This story repeated itself a number of times. Each time, D would end up in a different foster home only to exasperate the foster mother and then accuse the foster mother of abusing her. This would result in the child being sent back to her mother. The cycle completed itself usually within a week. After a few cycles of this, the child protective agency became exasperated with D. In their frustration, they agreed that they would bring the child to see me five times per week if I could stop this back and forth between foster homes and mother.

For this child, the psychic equivalent and the pretend mode of thinking seemed to be operating in an unsafe way. What happened in D's mind seemed to get translated to reality, although there was a pretend quality to it. As much as D was the author of this process, she was also a victim, and clearly stated that she did not like it. Underlying the case is something that I only became aware of after D left treatment with me. I reveal this so the problem she was struggling with in reality can be more clearly illustrated. Shortly after D was conceived, her mother and father went their separate ways. D only met her father a few times during her life. Her mother married another man with whom she had a son three years younger than D. The stepfather and mother clearly favored this boy who would at times parade about the house naked, waving his penis around, taunting D and saying in essence, "I have a penis and you do not."

When D began to see me, she clearly loved coming to her appointments. She enjoyed the attention I provided and would display herself by standing atop my desk pretending to be a beauty queen and dancing. At first, she was easily able to avoid stepping on my computer that sat at one end of the long desktop. However, she soon became jealous of the time I was not with her. She asked about everything in my office including the computer and learned that I spent time working on the computer when I was not with her. She then began to threaten the safety of the computer and keyboard that was at the end of her runway. When it became clear that she was determined to step on my keyboard, I placed the desktop off limits.

She became furious at me and for session after session she attempted to hit me. Initially this appeared as play. But as time progressed, the kicks, punches, and thrown objects came with more and more force in my direction and specifically targeting my groin. At the time, I was unaware of the situation at home with her brother and her intense jealousy and rage in regard to him. I asked her questions and wondered with her about her actions. I speculated, but only in a general way since I did not know enough specifics. I was unable to reflect back to her anything that she recognized. The attacks became worse. Finally, one day when she nearly hit her target, I became exasperated with her and I blurted out in sudden recognition, "Oh, I see. You are angry at me because you feel I have something that you do not." Suddenly, she had a look of surprise on her face as her jaw fell open during a period of stunned silence on both our parts. Then a look of anger swept over her, she straightened up, headed toward the door and just before she walked out and slammed it she said, "You ain't got nothing." I had reflected back something she recognized, but the reflection was not safe for her.

She reluctantly came back to see me the next day with her mother accompanying her, and I talked with her about how what I said was mean (she would not let me get away with saying that I felt mean), that there were differences between boys and girls but that girls had special things about them, that she had shown me how special she was and that I wanted to help her. The next session she came alone and began to talk about the terrible feelings she had about herself. The session after that she then began to complain that I made her have bad feelings. She told me that I was the source of the bad feelings. After a number of sessions in which she repeatedly ran out of my office to find her mother, I had her mother again join us in the office. With her mother in the room, I was able to say to her that I understood that she felt bad, but that she had had these bad feeling before, even when I was not around. I understood that coming to my office reminded her of these feelings but I told her that I would work with her to make it so that she did not feel so bad.

For several sessions, thereafter, she came alone and did not run out of the office, but she began to position herself between the doorframe and the door, and would then try to close the door with half of her inside the room and the other half outside the room. We talked about her dilemma in terms of understanding about her feeling being inside her and how I had helped her find these bad feelings. Now we needed to find a way of making it so these feelings were not so painful. We then began to write stories together including a classic family romance (Freud, 1908) in which D's mother and father were really a King and Queen, but they had mistakenly left her in someone else's care. In the story, after a number of challenges, D was reunited with her true King father and Queen mother. These stories seemed to bring her some relief.

Sometime after that, the cab driver who dropped her off at my office everyday left her at a place that she did not recognize. She wandered around for thirty minutes becoming increasingly more anxious. A security guard found her crying. She told the officer she needed to be with Dr. Fallon. When she was brought to me, she told me about her adventure and her fear of being lost and said she had repeatedly tried to picture me and imagine what it was like being with me to make her feel less anxious.

Toward the end of our time together, she summed up our work in this way: She drew a picture of a city with crooked buildings, windows, and doors in odd places. She then commented, "This is a crazy city.

This is where I live. You and I went there. It was safe to go together—you and me. You made it safe."

In this case, D began the treatment having little understanding of thoughts and feelings as separate from the outside world, operating in the psychic equivalent/pretend mode dichotomy. In this setting, her psychic equivalent and pretend mode repeatedly collided in an unsafe intrapsychic experience. At the beginning of our work, she was safely able to operate in the pretend mode by being a dancer and a beauty queen. However, when reality intervened and I was moved to protect my computer, I was challenged to create a safe environment in which all aspects of D were treated respectfully. When I tripped over (and reflected back to her) her understanding of reality (I had a penis and she did not) and all the meanings this had for her, she could not bear it and ran out of the room. In Dr. Benjamin's words, 'the third' collapsed. In the psychic equivalent mode, it was too dangerous. In Erikson's (1940) view, there was a play disruption. With the used of her mother, we were able to re-establish 'the third.'

With each successive cycle of challenge, collapse of 'the third' and resumption of 'the third,' more and more of her became a part of the work of co-creating 'the third.' My work in repeatedly reflecting back to her experience, including her experience of me, my finding a way to make these reflections safe (sometimes after the fact) gradually allowed these two modes to operate safely together. In her final drawing, she was able to verbalize this and demonstrate her developmental gain of self-reflection/mentalization in an abstract way with the city symbolizing her mind.

CONCLUSION

In this discussion, I have presented a fragment of an analysis of a child that demonstrates the concepts of and phenomena as Dr. Benjamin has described them. I have also attempted to overlay Dr. Benjamin's concepts with a developmental framework that used the concepts of core self, psychic equivalent and pretend modes of thinking and self-reflection/mentalization. This synthesis of Dr. Benjamin's concepts with Fonagy's developmental framework informs both child and adult psychoanalytic theory and technique.

REFERENCES

Ashington, J. and A. Gopnik. 1988. Children's understanding of representational change and its relation to the understanding of false belief and the appearance-reality distinction. *Child Development* 59: 26–37.

Bretherton, I. and M. Beeghly. 1982. Talking about internal states: the acquisition of an explicit theory of mind. *Developmental Psychology* 6: 906–921.

Erikson, E. H. 1940. Studies in the interpretation of play: I. clinical observation of play disruption in young children. *Genetic Psychology Monographs* XXII: 557–671.

Fonagy, P. and M. Target. 1996. Playing with reality: I. theory of mind and the normal development of psychic reality. *International Journal of Psychoanalysis* 77: 217–233.

———. 1998. Mentalization and the changing aims of child psychoanalysis. *Psychoanalytic Dialogues* 8: 87–114.

Freud, S. 1908. Family romances. *Standard Edition* IX: 237–241.

Klauber, J. 1987. The role of illusion in the psychoanalytic cure. *Illusion and Spontaneity in Psychoanalysis*. London: Free Association Books.

Klein, M. 1935. A contribution to the psychogenesis of manic-depressive states. *International Journal of Psychoanalysis* 16: 145–174.

———. 1940. Mourning and its relation to manic-depressive states. *International Journal of Psychoanalysis* 21: 125–153.

———. 1946. Notes on Some Schizoid Mechanisms. *International Journal of Psychoanalysis* 27: 99–110.

Parens, H. 1991. A view of the development of hostility in early life. *Journal of the American Psychoanalytic Association* 39: 75–108.

Seligman, S. 1999. Integrating Kleinian theory and intersubjectivity in infant research. *Psychoanalytic Dialogues* 9: 129–159.

Stern, D. 1985. *The Interpersonal World of the Infant*. New York: Basic Books.

Winnicott, D.W. 1949. Hate in the counter-transference. *International Journal of Psychoanalysis* 30: 69–74.

———. 1953. Transitional objects and transitional phenomena: a study of the first 'not-me' possession. *International Journal of Psychoanalysis* 34: 89–97.

———. 1960. The theory of the parent-infant relationship. *International Journal of Psychoanalysis* 41: 585–595.

6

Listening, Dreaming, Sharing

On the Uses of the Analyst's Inner Experiences

Theodore J. Jacobs, M.D.

I want to begin this contribution by relating a story concerning a long-running argument that I had with a distinguished colleague, someone whom I much admired, for, among other things, his remarkable clinical skills. This story, in fact, involves a clinical moment and farther on I'll relate other clinical examples, one of which involves an uncontrolled, unthought out enactment of mine that grew out of the sheer frustration that I was experiencing in trying to work with an angry, bitter, and profoundly stubborn man. This was an individual who announced at the beginning of treatment that he was simultaneously taking on his third wife and third analyst. And, he added, he had little expectation that either of these relationships would work out.

In describing these situations, I hope to illustrate what I regard as an important aspect of the listening process; or, more specifically, of attunement; the heart—and soul as well—of analytic listening. I hope to demonstrate, or at least encourage the reader to consider, the idea that empathic attunement involves a good deal more than careful, attentive listening and the capacity to imagine oneself into the mind of another person, as important as these qualities are. In its richest and most valuable form—the condition we aim for as analysts—it involves creations on the part of the analyst; that is, fantasies, memories, reveries, sparks of intuition, daydreams, and, as I will describe, sometimes actual dreams as well. These are, or should be, inherent parts of evocative listening.

I would also like to suggest that such inner experiences do not arise equally under all conditions of analytic listening. In fact, they may be retarded or actually inhibited by particular ways of listening. I will return to this point later on in the chapter.

Let me turn now to my long-running dispute with my good friend, Dr. Y. A brilliant clinician with a sharp, incisive mind and a truly remarkable talent for grasping outcroppings of the unconscious as they appear in syntax and phrasing, simile and metaphor, he was by nature and inclination a scientist who approached analytic work in that spirit. While recognizing that the analyst's subjectivity can provide useful cues to unconscious conflicts in the patient, he always insisted on a careful searching of the analytic material for corroborative evidence.

Dr. Y saw little value in all the commotion about countertransference, enactments, intersubjectivity and the like that we hear so much about today. He viewed countertransference, as did Freud (1912) and Annie Reich (1951) before him, primarily as representing the stirring of ghosts in the analyst and, therefore, as constituting an impediment to correct understanding. He deplored what he viewed as the unjustified elevation of countertransference to a special place in our field, a place where it was held to be on a par with, or even to replace, dreams and free association as a superior, and more accessible, road to the unconscious.

While I agreed with much of what Dr. Y had to say, I put more stock in the analyst's subjective experiences, holding that they often tell us something about both patient and analyst—and the interactions between them—that otherwise is difficult to grasp. Dr. Y liked to tease me about my views, and once, after I had given a talk in which at some length, I described how, in a session, I used my inner experiences to detect a countertransference feeling of which I had been unaware, he came up to me. "That was interesting, Ted, he said with a smile on his face, "but somehow I had the impression that psychoanalysis is about the psychology of the patient."

We went on that way for a number of years, each holding to his own view and believing that the other was short sighted, when one evening at a social gathering, Dr. Y took me aside. "I want to tell you about an experience I had with a patient," he began, "I think you will be interested." Dr. Y then described an incident that took place during his work with a highly obsessional man who was terrified of his feelings and who spoke in a flat, unemotional, and abstract manner. His defensive style and muted personality made him very difficult to listen to and, in one session just prior to a holiday break in the treatment, Dr. Y fell asleep for perhaps a minute or two. While asleep he had the following dream: He was in a railway station some place in Europe. A train pulls in and his aged father gets off. They happily greet each other on the platform, embrace, and Dr. Y's father gets back on the train, which then departs. At that point Dr. Y awoke and realized what this dream was telling him.

The dream closely duplicated an actual occurrence that had taken place some years previously. Dr. Y had been traveling in Europe and, had, in fact, met his father at a railway station. As in the dream, they embraced and spent some time together. Then Dr. Y's father departed on another train. That was the last time that Dr. Y saw his father alive. He died a few weeks later. Why did Dr. Y have this dream? It was, he realized, a communication about what was transpiring in the session and, particularly, about feelings that his patient was struggling to ward off. Despite himself, the patient has begun to feel warmly toward Dr. Y and was experiencing a sense of loss at the fact that they would not see each other for some time. These emotions, however, he could not express. He protected himself against them by veering off into a vague and general description of a social event that he had recently attended. Put off and frustrated by his patient's monotonous recital and not yet able to grasp what was happening, Dr. Y fell asleep. His dream, then, spoke for him, telling him through its depiction of the farewell scene with his own father what threatening emotions the patient was seeking to keep at bay.

Dr. Y did not tell the patient that he had fallen asleep and had this dream, but he was able to use what arose from within to help his patient come in touch, not only with what he was experiencing, but with the underlying fears that caused him to have to ward off his affection for Dr. Y.

Ending his account, Dr. Y gave me a warm smile. "I guess you have a point," he said, "I still disagree with you, but it looks like my unconscious is on your side.

I relate this story not to prove the correctness of my views—there is plenty of room for disagreement as to the role of the analyst's psychology in treatment—but to raise certain questions about the analyst's inner experiences.

FOUR IMPORTANT QUESTIONS

1) Are all of the analyst's inner experiences, all of the dreams, daydreams, fantasies, and memories that arise as we work meaningfully related to the patient's material? Is it true, as the early Kleinians maintained, that there is a pipeline from the unconscious of the patient to the unconscious of the analyst and that whatever appears in the analyst's mind is placed there, as it were, by the patient through the process of projective identification? Or are many of these experiences instances of countertransference responses primarily related to aspects of the analyst's history and conflicts that are evoked by the patient's material?

2) How do the analyst's subjective experiences relate to questions of empathy and attunement, issues that most concern us today?

3) Does the way we work, and, indeed, the way we think about analysis affect the extent to which inner experiences are evoked in, and can be grasped by, the analyst?

4) Is there any place for sharing aspects of our inner experiences with patients? Or should we strive at all times to use our subjective experiences only as raw material to craft interpretations?

Answers to all of these questions are hard to come by—if, indeed, there are answers at all. In any case, I surely do not have them. What I will try to offer are some thoughts, a bit of clinical material, a report on some relevant research findings, a piece of pertinent history, and a lot of speculation.

Let me begin by citing some fascinating work carried out by Dr. Morton Reiser, a skilled analyst and a renowned researcher in the area of neurophysiology.

Through the use of modern brain imaging techniques, Dr. Reiser (1997) discovered that the analyst's memories of what the patient tells him; that is, all of the patient's material, including her history, her concerns, and her conflicts, are stored in the same area of the brain—as are the analyst's memories of, and fantasies about, his own life experiences.

These memory circuits interweave and overlap, so that if the analyst is listening well and in a particular way—this is a matter that I will return to shortly—it is highly likely that the memories, the images, the daydreams and, as we have seen, even the dreams that arise in the analyst's mind, will do so in connection with, and often in anticipation of, material of the patient's that is on the cusp of consciousness. Often it is the registration, outside of awareness, in the analyst's mind of thoughts, memories, and fantasies concealed within, and unconsciously alluded to in the patient's material that stimulates corresponding memories or fantasies in the analyst. What Dr. Reiser's work has given us, then, is some impressive scientific support for the idea, articulated long ago by Freud, that unconscious communication between patient and analyst is an ongoing process in every analysis.

OTTO ISAKOWER AND THE ANALYTIC INSTRUMENT

Freud left others to explore this terrain and the person who did so most creatively and, to my mind, most importantly, was Otto Isakower, whose imaginative concept of the "analytic instrument" (1963a) is, unfortunately, not well understood by many analysts.

Not a few colleagues, for instance, believe that the concept pictures the analyst as a neutral, anonymous, scientific observer and that it ignores, or by inference, denies the importance in clinical work of the analyst's subjectivity.

This is just the reverse of what Isakower (1965) had in mind when he outlined his views in a talk to the faculty of the New York Psychoanalytic Institute. Isakower's concept—to be understood as a metaphorical way of articulating the remarkable, and remarkably intimate, connection between the minds of patient and analyst that can develop in an analytic hour—speaks to a level of attunement, a level of empathic grasping of unconscious transmissions, that is an essential, but in today's world often neglected, aspect of the analytic process.

The analytic instrument does not refer to the analyst, but to a joint creation of patient and analyst. Assembled in, and existing only, during the analytic hour, it might concretely be imagined as a brain containing two halves. One half belongs to the patient, the other half to the analyst. In the analytic session, as both analyst and patient loosen their ties to the external world and enter into a slightly altered state of consciousness—essentially the condition of daydreaming—these two halves come together in a temporary union, a bridge is built, and unconscious messages can flow between them. In this state of mind, which the analyst must consciously employ—and, arguably, due in large measure to this state of mind—it is highly likely that the analyst's subjective experiences will be meaningfully, and importantly, related to communications from the patient.

It is as though, in a remarkably intuitive way, Isakower anticipated Reiser's finding that mental representations of the inner world of patient and analyst, as well as their neuronal correlates, interweave and overlap in the brain of the analyst so that if we work in a way that allows us access to them, we can utilize ourselves to grasp aspects of the unconscious mind that have an ongoing influence on the lives of our patients.

If you had been as student in Isakower's classes, as I had the privilege of being in the 1960s, you would have encountered a remarkable individual. Quite a small man—Isakower was probably no more than five-three, weighing perhaps 120 pounds, he had the most sensitive ear for the tones and overtones, the music of an hour, of anyone I have ever known.

Attuned to the harmonies—and the discords—of a session, Isakower was aware of momentary visual images, of fragments, of poetry or song, or an unbidden memory making an unexpected appearance. Sometimes he would share these experiences, noting that such and such an image had arisen in his mind and inquiring if this stirred any response in the patient. Quite surprising—at least to me—was how often the image, the odd phrase, the scrap of memory, was related to some piece of history, or some emerging fantasy in the patient.

Although he could be a terror in the classroom—he did not suffer fools gladly—Isakower also had a wry sense of humor. At one time he was put on a committee of the Institute whose other members were seven powerful women. It is an interesting piece of history that in the fifties and sixties, the New York Institute was run by women, many of whom were distinguished contributors to psychoanalysis; Edith Jacobson, Marianne Kris, Dora Hartman, Ruth Eissler, Lillian Malcove, and Mary O'Neil Hawkins, to mention a few. Noting this overwhelmingly female composition of the committee, a friend of Isakower's inquired as to what it was like for him to work with this group.

"How is it for you, Otto," he asked. "To be the only man on a committee with seven such powerful women?" Isakower shrugged his shoulders in what was clearly a gesture of resignation, "Well, I tell you," he said, "It is simply a case of seven Snow Whites and the Dwarf."

As I mentioned, a very important part of the analytic instrument is the set of mind of the analyst. This fact is often neglected today in discussions of technique. Freud (1912) spoke of this early on when he said that the analyst must set his mind as the receiving apparatus in a telephone is attuned to its transmitting part. This set of mind involves a deliberate shift in the direction of reverie and daydreaming. It is a conscious effort to attune oneself to the music of the hour, just as one might do at a concert as one allows one's mind to drift, and register the themes of a symphony.

Hopefully, the patient can enter into a comparable state of mind. He or she will not do this, by the way, without help, guidance, and explanation concerning this aspect of the analytic process. Not to offer assistance in this way—some colleagues pride themselves on not mentioning the fundamental rule, no less more detailed explanations—is comparable to a tennis pro expecting a novice to hit a smooth forehand without having taught him how to hold a racquet.

For unconscious transmissions to be accurately and usefully grasped by the analyst, then, the analytic instrument must be set right. When it is, the conditions for a special kind of connection are in place and, unlike the unhappy couple in the Chinese proverb who are lying in the same bed dreaming different dreams, analyst and patient, each in their place, are daydreaming dreams that are, in fact, connected. And it is this connection; this special relationship of two minds, that allows for a level of empathy and attunement that is in touch with the imaginative creations of the mind that not only are outside of awareness, but beyond the level of empathy that we ordinarily refer to when we use that word.

In usual discourse, we describe empathy as the imaginative feat of putting oneself in another's shoes, of walking a mile in the other fellow's moccasins as in an American Indian saying. As we know, this capacity is vitally important to treatment. Schwaber (1983; 1986; 1990; 1992) has amply demonstrated this in her superb writings. But this level of empathy is attained largely through an act of the imagination that is pretty much a conscious phenomenon. We think and feel our way into the other's life and world. We enter into what is called a trial identification. This process may, of course, lead to an important connection and the beginning of the kind of receptivity to transmissions that is invaluable in analysis. But unless the instrument is properly calibrated, this receptivity is likely to be incomplete, partially blocked, or not possible at all.

SOME RECENT ADVANCES

These issues are relevant to current practice. In recent years, as we are well aware, there has been much focus on the transference, the here-and-now, enactments, and the interaction of patient and analyst. We have been taught to grasp the interactive moment, to listen for transference material, and to work actively with implicit memories that reveal themselves in specific behaviors in the analytic hour. This has been a genuine advance. We are much better than we used to be at picking up, and working effectively, with the dance—and the movements of the dance—between analyst and patient.

But this advance has come at a price—in my view quite a heavy price—for often it requires a focusing of the mind, a keen awareness of the moment that precludes the kind of regressive movement, the slight alteration of consciousness, the loosening of bonds, that allows the analyst to be in a creatively receptive place.

Even the well-established technique of evenly hovering attention is not employed as readily as it once was. For many analysts it has given way to the kind of presence, the kind of attentiveness that is characteristic of conversation and dialogue. And if utilized in such a way that hovering attention hovers over the field of action, ever alert to the moves and counter-moves of patient and analyst, it may not include the crucial element, the easing back of the mind, the opening of our ordinary barriers to what Christopher Bollas (1987) has called 'news from within.'

Today our conception of the analytic instrument includes more than it did in Isakower's original description. Isakower said nothing about the visual element and its role in analysis, nothing about the way the analyst uses her eyes as well as her ears. In recent years we have become aware of how important open-ended observation is in analysis, how much information is obtained by allowing oneself to look as well as to listen and to let the streams of visual information intermingle and interweave with that which comes to us through the auditory sphere.

Years ago Annie Reich taught me not to place my chair behind the couch, a position which allows the analyst to see almost nothing of the patient's body, but at an angle so that it is possible to observe posture, gesture, and movement in the patient, all vital sources of information. One of the great challenges facing analysts today, in fact, is for analysts to learn not only to observe the nonverbal, but to integrate the complex language of the body with the words spoken by patient and analyst.

Let me now turn to a brief clinical example as an illustration of the way that, using the analytic instrument, the memories and fantasies that surface in the mind of the analyst may help illuminate preconscious material in the patient that is rising toward consciousness. Insight gained in this way may also convey a level of empathy and attunement that fosters the unfolding of the analytic process.

A CLINICAL ILLUSTRATION

One day at the beginning of an analytic hour Mr. D, a verbal and articulate man in his forties, was unusually silent. For several minutes he lay, almost motionless on the couch. I had noticed as he entered the office that he seemed sad and now I thought I saw a small tear forming in the corner of one eye. After a few minutes Mr. D began to make slight rotating movements with his arms, which he held in front of his face. It was as if he was sitting behind the wheel of a car and turning it slightly one way, then another. Observing my patient acting in this manner on the couch, and saying nothing, I felt quite totally lost. I did not know what to make of behavior that was clearly unusual for Mr. D.

The silence continued and as I watched and waited, my mind drifted. At first nothing seemed to arise from within. Then a strange image appeared. It was of a wreck of a car, a beat up Desoto model that I owned as a college student. I bought it, I think, for four hundred dollars and it looked worth half the price, with a dented hood, a gashed fender, and a paint job that had the effect of evoking nausea in even casual passers by. I nicknamed this vehicle the Tan Terror and there it was in my daydream.

Then something else arose in my mind. It was the sudden recollection of an event in Mr. D's adolescence that he had related to me several years before. I remember being touched by what Mr. D had told me then, but for some reason we had not explored its meaning at that time. Now the event surfaced and, in response, I uttered a single phrase to Mr. D: "The senior prom." Immediately Mr. D responded with a sound that seemed half laugh, half cry. And full of feelings, he again related the story to me. This time we talked a great deal about this incident and what it signified in his life. What happened was this.

As a teenager, Mr. D was pretty miserable. Overweight, nearsighted and plagued by acne, he was not very popular with girls and felt himself an outsider at his high school. When it came time for the senior prom, Mr. D found himself desperate. He simply could not get a date, and for him not to go to the prom would be a humiliating defeat. As a last ditch effort to find someone to go with, Mr. D called a girl whom he barely knew and made her an offer she could not refuse. If she would agree to be his date for the evening, they would arrive in style as celebrities. They would make their appearance in a police cruiser, complete with siren and flashing lights. Mr. D's, father, a police sergeant in the small town in which they lived, had promised to obtain an off-duty patrol car for the evening and, for a few hours, to be the couple's chauffer.

The girl accepted this offer and when the time came, Mr. D outfitted in his rented tux and carrying the mandatory orchid, waited for his father to arrive from the station house. You can imagine how Mr. D felt when, instead of appearing in the promised patrol car, his father drove up in the family's eight year old, battered station wagon. Due to an emergency, all the squad cars were in use, and none could be spared. Mr. D was crushed, his hope for a moment of glory—a moment to redeem himself in the eyes of his classmates, thoroughly dashed.

Clearly important in its own right, in time this experience came to stand for much of Mr. D's adolescence and, especially, for all of the frustrations and disappointments that he experienced in his relationship with a quixotic and troubled father. The recovery and working through of the impact of this relationship on Mr. D played a central role in his analysis.

What had taken place here? How did it happen that an image of my first car, the Tan Terror, arose in my mind, followed by a memory of Mr. D's painful adolescent experience? That morning I had been unable to drive to work in my regular car as it was in the shop for repairs. Instead, I was forced to take the old, rather beat up sedan that

I kept around the house for just such situations. When I drove by my office in search of a parking spot, I noticed Mr. D at the front door just about to enter. I was not certain, but I thought that he spotted my car as it passed by. In fact, Mr. D did catch a glimpse of me in the battered sedan and immediately he experienced a feeling of keen disappointment. He had pictured me as—and prided himself on being connected to—a prosperous analyst who undoubtedly drove a stylish BMW. And there I was in the latest, and not much improved, incarnation of the Tan Terror.

What Mr. D was not aware of was the connection that, unconsciously, he made to the senior prom experience and the crushing disappointment at the hands of his father. Being disappointed by me, his father in the transference, evoked that prior episode and he made reference to both through the unusual driving movements that he carried out on the couch and by means of the sudden sadness that came over him.

For my part, the combination of my driving the old, beat up car and observing Mr. D's mood and behavior on the couch stirred memories both of Mr. D's adolescent experience and, my own very different, but relevant, experience, at age eighteen, with a wreck of a car that I was ashamed of. This connection put me in touch with, and helped Mr. D and me understand, an experience that stood for much in his life; one that had arisen in a rather casual way some years before, but had not been sufficiently explored.

Would all of this material have come up in the analysis at some other time and through some other means? I do not know. Very possibly it would have, but it also might not have. All I can say for sure is that for me, in this instance, the use of the analytic instrument and the inner experience it helped evoke, proved to be enormously useful.

What I have described thus far are various levels of empathy and attunement, from ones that lie closer to consciousness and involve imagining oneself into the shoes of another to that kind of empathic attunement that allows us to grasp unconscious communications from our patients. This latter mode of attunement, one that I believe requires a special way of listening, is uniquely valuable in psychoanalysis, which deals first and foremost with the influence of the unconscious mind and that has sometimes been called the science of traces.

SHARING ONE'S INNER EXPERIENCE WITH PATIENTS

But what about the question of disclosing or, as I prefer, sharing aspects of our inner experiences with patients? Is such sharing useful or disruptive to the analytic process? Should it be considered a countertransference enactment, used more to relieve tension in the analyst than to help the patient? Or should sharing, in some cases, be considered an integral part of the empathic experience? In all situations, in other words, is empathy expressed indirectly in the usual fashion, through tone, manner, and appropriate utterances, as valuable as a more direct expression of the analyst's subjective experiences?

Needless to say no one has definitive answers to such questions. In my opinion they must be determined on an individual basis without prior bias as to how one must view the matter of disclosure and without being harnessed to fixed ideas of what is proper and correct in analytic technique.

At the time that Isakower (1963a; 1963b) shared some of his inner experiences with patients this way of working was unheard of. It was viewed as inappropriate self-disclosure, an absolute taboo at the time, and were it not for the fact that Isakower had such stature in the field, he would have been soundly criticized as an exhibitionist and worse.

Currently it is Christopher Bollas (1987) who is perhaps the most articulate spokesman for the idea that putting forward aspects of one's subjective experiences allows the patient to get in touch with, and to integrate, projected and warded off parts of himself. His is a cogent argument, well put, and, to me, quite convincing. But I would like to suggest that in some situations there may be another reason to share some of what one is experiencing. For certain patients, I have found, sharing is necessary for them to trust, to take in, and to make use of the analyst's empathic understanding.

Let me offer a brief example of what I mean by describing some impulsive, out of control behavior on my part that led to a surprising result.

ANOTHER CLINICAL ILLUSTRATION

For a number of years I was working—or trying to work—in an analysis with a man who lived his life knotted up with rage and frustration. When angry, which was a good deal of the time, he lay on the couch scrunched into what seemed like a dense and tight human ball, silent and unapproachable.

In this behavior, Mr. K mimicked his father, a bitter and angry man who had lost an arm in an industrial accident when still a teenager. For the rest of his life the father remained a wounded man, isolated and withdrawn, furious over his fate, and ready to lash out at others for the cruel blow that had befallen him. At night the father would often sit alone in the living room with the lights out, smoking a cigarette, lost in thought and memories. Mr. K remembered the utter futility he felt when, as a child, he tried to approach this lonely figure. Folded into himself, barely noticing the boy who shyly tried to speak to him, the father was totally unreachable.

As you would predict, Mr. K, as an adult, became a man very much like his father. He too, was a lonely, isolated, and angry person who kept very much to himself. As I mentioned, in analysis his anger took the form of silent withdrawal, with Mr. K very much folded into himself. I interpreted Mr. K's behavior in every way you can imagine—and then some. I spoke of his identification with his father, the rage at being abandoned, his protective withdrawal, you name it. Every relevant intervention was offered at one time or another, all without much effect.

At one point in the analysis I had to be away for a few days and when I returned for Mr. K's early morning appointment, I was not in the best of moods. I had had little sleep, and was tired and out of sorts. Mr. K greeted me in the usual way, with stony silence and with his oyster-like withdrawal. For my part, I duly interpreted his anger at my abandoning him, his wish to retaliate, his withdrawal in the face of his own aggression and a lot more. Mr. K's only response was to pull further into himself. As I sat there in this gray silence, I felt totally frustrated, totally helpless, filled with rising anger myself. And before I knew what was happening, I found myself speaking. "I would like to share something with you," I said, hearing my words as though they belonged to some alien creature. "I am sitting here in this silence feeling totally alone, totally shut out, totally helpless. It is as though a wall of steel has come between us, a wall that can never be breached. No matter what I say or do, you do not respond. I feel as though I am speaking into a void, to a man so enclosed, so removed that there is no way, no possible way, of reaching him. And do you know something else," I went on, "I feel in my gut, as I have not felt before, what it must have been like for you to try to reach out to that lonely figure sitting in darkness, that angry, knotted up man who could not and would not be reached. For at this moment you are the man and I am the little boy."

To my amazement, Mr. K, this iron tough street fighter, broke into tears and wept for fully five minutes. When he recovered he spoke softly. "I don't know what happened there," he said, "something broke inside of me. It was not what you said, you've said more or less the same thing many times before. It was that it was you speaking your feelings, not just an interpretation, not just words. I knew for the first time that you really understood from inside, from your feelings, what it was like for me. I am funny that way. I am a SOB and I don't trust words. Words are too easy. I can only trust someone when I know that he has been there, has felt what I feel. Before you said all the right things, but this was different. This was a different kind of understanding."

If this was true, if my response was not simply a piece of acting out of frustration and aggression—which it certainly was—where did it come from? Was there, I wondered, any deeper source in myself? What was at the root of a comment that followed none of the rules of good technique?

That night after dinner, as I was thinking about what had happened, I remembered something that I had not thought about for probably fifty years; that as a boy I would sometimes enter our apartment and sense that someone was there, sitting in the dark, not smoking, but chewing on a cigarette as men who liked to chew tobacco sometimes did in those days.

This man was my grandfather, an extraordinarily silent man, someone who I very much wanted to, but never did, get to know. He would often sit silently in the dark, musing, thinking. A kindly and gentle person—he would say a few words of greeting and hand me a stick of gum or a couple of nickels when I tried to talk to him—he nonetheless remained, in his own way, as distant and mysterious as was Mr. K's father.

My experience of frustration with a silent and removed man whom I longed to, but could not, know must unconsciously, have contributed to the intensity of my reaction. I had no idea of this, but recognizing it later helped me appreciate how often in analysis unconscious connections to our unique, but parallel life experiences help fuel both our invaluable gut reactions, and our overreactions, to our patients.

This incident took place five or six years ago and I have been thinking about it since. Does it tell us anything? This was different, Mr. K said, a different kind of understanding. Understanding, from the gut, visceral understanding that somehow got put into words, and was shared with the patient.

As I thought about what happened with Mr. K, I came to understand that he needed my openness, my directness, my passion, to believe, to trust, to know that I knew. Was he one of a kind, someone whose history and personality required—and induced—such a spontaneous and uncontrolled intervention? The answer, I think, is yes, and possibly no. Mr. K may not be alone. In fact, in the years since this happened I have seen several patients who, before they can feel fully understand, need to know that the analyst understands not only with words, but with resonant feelings. These experiences have caused me to ask myself if, in some cases, at least, the analyst's empathy needs to be quite openly communicated and that for it to be accepted, truly taken in and not kept at an unhelpful remove, we need to share some of our inner experiences with these patients.

Such individuals are usually those, like Mr. K, who have come to distrust words and language, and who may have experienced deception or multiple disappointments at the hands of others. They are also people who themselves use words to obfuscate as much as to communicate. And they are individuals who take poorly to signs of withholding, avoidance, or evasion on the part of the analyst, all of which they equate with dishonesty and deception. These are patients who, to move forward in analysis, may need to know that the analyst is with them in ways that they can understand. Interpretation of this quality, at least for quite a while, does not suffice. During this period, to reach the patient, the analyst must meet certain of their fundamental needs. This kind of situation, and all of the questions it raises, require, I believe, a good deal more study and exploration.

CONCLUSION

Let me, then, summarize very briefly what I have tried to communicate. *First*, I believe that empathy and attunement are at the heart, not only of analytic listening, but of the analytic process itself. *Second*, empathy and attunement are descriptive words that refer, not to one, but to a variety of, processes in analysis. Some of these involve conscious experience, other experiences that lie outside of awareness. Among the latter, unconscious communication between analyst and patient is a crucial and central aspect of analytic treatment. Such communication can most fully and usefully be grasped when the analyst and patient enter into a state of mind that allows for reverie and daydreaming.

Finally, I suggest that for certain patients, direct communication of the analyst's inner experiences, particularly those that convey empathic understanding, may be necessary for the analyst's healing empathy to be accepted, internalized, and made an integral part of the therapeutic experience.

REFERENCES

Bollas, C. 1987. *The Shadow of the Object.* New York: Columbia University Press.

Freud, S. 1912. Recommendations to physicians practicing psychoanalysis. *Standard Edition* 12: 111–120.

Isakower, O. 1963a. Minutes of New York Psychoanalytic Institute faculty meeting, October 14, unpublished.

———. 1963b. Minutes of New York Psychoanalytic Institute faculty meeting, November 20, unpublished.

Reich, A. 1951. On countertransference. *International Journal of Psychoanalysis* 41: 389–395.

Reiser, M. 1997. The art and science of dream interpretation: Isakower revisited. *Journal of the American Psychoanalytic Association* 45: 891–906.

Schwaber, E. 1983. Psychoanalytic listening and psychic reality. *International Review of Psychoanalysis* 10: 379–392.

———. 1986. Reconstruction and perceptual experience. *Journal of the American Psychoanalytic Association* 34: 911–932.

———. 1990. Interpretation and the therapeutic action of psychoanalysis. *International Journal of Psychoanalysis* 71: 229–240.

———. 1992. Countertransference: the analyst's retreat from the patient's vantage point. *International Journal of Psychoanalysis* 73: 349–362.

7

LISTENING, READING, AND THE 'IN-BETWEEN' SPACE

Discussion of Jacobs's Chapter "Listening, Dreaming, Sharing: On the Uses of the Analyst's Inner Experience"

David M. Sachs, M.D.

"I want to begin my discussion by relating a story concerning a long-running conversation I had with a distinguished colleague someone whom I much admired, for among other things, his remarkable clinical skills." Sounds familiar? In case you have forgotten, let me remind you that this was the first sentence of Dr. Ted Jacobs's contribution, which is the focus of my discussion.

My story, however, is not about Dr. Y., Dr. Jacobs's "distinguished colleague," but about Ted himself. It began over thirty years ago when we were members of an intensive study group that met twice a year. During that period I heard Ted present similar clinical material of his own as well as discuss the clinical materials of the other members. On this basis I began to imagine what Ted would say today and thought I could guess the subject matter and the style of his paper. Confident that an empathic moment was occurring, I associated to the song "Accentuate the Positive" and considered giving my discussion the title "Do Mess with Mr. In-Between." As you have just heard Ted creates pieces of analysis that depend upon the interactive participation of the analysand's unconscious with Ted's unconscious, a space "in-between" the two participants. In making this public he illustrates how he is in dialogue with his unconscious at the same time that he is discovering what prevents his analysand from being in a similar dialogue. For many decades this space was a blank page in the analytic literature. Instead, the pages were filled with the analyst's description of the analysand's inner space and her difficulties in having the internal dialogue that occurs within Ted's mind. The belief in vogue then was that the analyst need not have an internal dialogue with his unconscious because he had permanently analyzed away all unconscious conflicts that might obtund his ability to analyze and then qualify him to write an objective narrative of the analysand's psyche. Memories that might block his response to his analysand supposedly had been dissolved by the laser beams of insight that his own analyst had directed at him to dissolve forever his internal conflicts. The analyst who became a "clear" could "accentuate the positive"; that is, function in a completely objective way like Star Trek's Mr. Spock. The analyst who could not become a "clear" is unable to "eliminate the negative"; that is, he functions in a nonobjective way and imposes his thoughts and feelings on the analysand. Instead of occupying either extreme, Ted carves out a vast middle ground in which much of the work of analyzing occurs. In this area lives Ted's idea of "attunement; the heart—and soul as well—of analytic listening." It is fair to say that Ted has been messing with the "in-between" much to the benefit of psychoanalysis.

LISTENING WHILE READING

In this discussion I would like to continue attuning myself to Ted's paper by making public my spontaneous, marginal notes made during my second reading. This represents my side of the conversation. I would like to include all of them but then I would then have a paper far longer than Ted's. Nor do I intend to boil down my notes to create an abstract version of my response. Instead I will select some of my responses to open the door to dialogue and will look forward to his reply during the discussion.

I suggest that my way of reading is similar to analytic listening. I am not reading Ted's paper as a concrete reality that contains all its meanings within it; nor am I reading his text as a screen upon which I can impose my private meanings with no regard for what he tells us.

The so-called "new school" of literary criticism suggests that the reader should assume all meanings are contained in the text. Others astutely observe the limitation of this approach by showing how different readers read the same text differently. They allege that if a book is read only once the reader always reads the same book because he silently imposes his own unconscious interpretations on the text. Only by knowing what is imposed on a text can the author's meaning and the reader's interpretations be teased apart. Analysts listen to the analysand in many, many "readings," and thereby create an analytic conversation with multiple levels of meaning that enable the listening and feeling analyst to separate the meanings that belong to the analyst from those that belong to the analysand. I will be doing to Ted's paper what he does with his analysands; namely provide a window opening onto the reader's side of the writer's text.

When I read about Dr. Y, I was surprised that Ted describes his clinical work as "brilliant" at the same time as he informs us that he rejects those advances in psychoanalysis on which Ted's work depends. Is it possible I asked myself, to view countertransference, enactments, and intersubjectivity as a "commotion" with little value? To answer my own question I decided that Dr. Y's brilliance might be understood as the ability to observe the analysand "without memory or desire," as Bion (1967) suggests. This stance would protect him from the emotions of transference and countertransference and enable him to analyze as if he is capable of being an objective observer of "syntax and phrasing, simile and metaphor." I used this immediate impression to confirm my initial opinion that Dr. Y is an exemplar of the old time Positivist "analyst/scientist" and even assumed he misunderstood the importance of his own dream when he concludes, "I still disagree with you (Ted), but it looks like my unconscious is on your side." To benefit from what the dream told him, I noted that he "should" have said, "I no longer disagree with you because I learned that my relationship with my own unconscious was not on the side of the analysand." Further stigmatizing Dr. Y, I reminded myself of the many analysts I knew who were trained after World War II whose blind spots continued throughout their careers as they tried to become better at being Mr. Spock. Although a talent for accurate, objective observation is an essential skill for an analyst to have, used exclusively it is not sufficient and becomes a liability. Unless joined by the skills Ted proposes it becomes a disservice to analysands. Annie Reich, a wonderful mentor for Ted and myself, spoke to this point (Reich, 1951) when she was one of the early American proponents of the value of learning from our countertransference. Her claim is simply that if countertransference doesn't happen, neither does an analysis. Unless Dr. Y comes to accept Ted's ideas as adding to his own, his analysand's are in danger of being asked to become objective observers of their own unconscious instead of participants in a conversation with it.

Ted then evokes images of Passover in asking his four questions. Unlike the Hagadah, he modestly claims not to have answers to his questions, as if there are answers. I thought, "Yes Ted you are right to wonder because they are not really questions. It is easier for me to think of them as statements that can generate discussions about how to make psychoanalysis a humane discipline being lived between two thinking, feeling remembering people." Then, I thought, "It is not an accident that these questions follow his discussion of his scientist friend Dr. Y whose view of science is mired in the nineteenth century." Perhaps, Ted is asking us to move beyond Dr. Y and consider seriously his belief that the work of a psychoanalyst cannot be reduced to the work of an observing scientist looking through his microscope at the interesting movements and excrescences of the patient. I hope Ted can help me understand his extremely high opinion of Dr. Y's clinical skills. By framing the discussion in terms of questions with answers, I thought that Ted gives too much room for Dr. Y to consider his questions to have answers that he can provide. But, I don't think Ted wants answers: he wants dialogue that he cannot have unless Dr. Y is willing to admit that he needs to continue to have an open conversation with his own unconscious. I thought, "Dr. Y would be unhappy to accept the idea that he is not a Mr. Spock and that he must continue to talk and listen to his own dynamic, never fully known unconscious."

The path of the organization of Ted's paper hits another detour from his own goal when he considers the excellent work of Reiser (1997). Much as I value the potential contribution of brain imaging, my immediate reaction was that it adds nothing to Ted's demonstration of the intricate psychological connections that are established in the brains of the analysand and the analyst as they spend hours communicating with each other. I hope Ted tells us why it matters that the neurons involved are "stored in the same area of the brain"? I thought that it is analogous to an art historian who does not care a fig that vision is processed in the occipital cortex when she is having a conversation with a painting? What matters is what she sees in a picture: what matters to an analysand is what Ted sees that she does not see and what matters to Ted is her response is to what he sees, etc., etc. And, it matters to Ted and myself if the reason we do not see is due to an emotional blind spot in ourselves that can be detected and used in the service of the analysand. In this sense we no longer have aspirations to be a Mr. Spock, but are happy to be in a lifelong conversation with our unconscious.

I found myself more attuned to Ted's beliefs when he turns away from being polite to Dr. Y and from seeking unnecessary support from Reiser (1997), and moves on to discuss the "analyzing instrument" (Isakower, 1963). Even though I find the metaphor an unhappy one because it has a mechanical feel that is not in the spirit of Ted's approach and quite at odds with the process of attunement. Since I prefer Ted's more accurate term of "evocative listening," I wonder why he suggests the awkward term Isakower chose. Later, in reflecting on my spontaneous response to the "analytic instrument" I realized that such an analogy has a spooky power to control the extensions of its meaning. For example, I thought the idea of an instrument used by both forces him to claim that it only exists in the analytic hour. In fact, he demonstrates that it exists outside the hour in his own thoughts of embarrassment at driving an old car. He is tuning his relationship to his own unconscious in preparation to becoming attuned to his analysand, forming the core of his insightful comments. In turn, the results are received by the analysand, modifying his relationship to his own unconscious. This process is ongoing in each, perhaps coming together at its maximum during an hour, but continuing separately.

I began to wonder if Ted would consider tuning two violins as a more suitable analogy for attunement? Violins are separate instruments that can be tuned to each other, and stay in tune when they leave the concert hall. Granted, they will need to be retuned, but this can happen in many venues. In my view of attunement, the Chinese couple dreaming different dreams need not be unhappy. Indeed, having different dreams provides the opportunity for retuning which is the "heart and soul" of the analytic process and happy living. I suspect Ted really is not unhappy when he is temporarily out of tune with his analysands. Only then, can he come into attunement by re-tuning and use that skill to help the analysand learn how to retune. That's the fun of analysis.

ATTUNEMENT AND OBJECTIVITY

I am sure you understand how much I value Ted's contribution to the messy "in-between" that is most of an analysis. But, I would feel remiss if I did not mention my concerns about the limits of the idea of attunement. To do so, I must return to Dr. Y and do justice to his position which I was beginning to recognize I had treated unfairly in my spontaneous responses. The psychoanalyst is not just an attuned listener and interpreter; she is also an objective observer. There are obdurate facts that comprise the history and contribute to the formation of a truthful narrative of our patients. Dr. Y, like Freud, is apparently a superb observer of these facts, possessing half of the skills an analyst needs to oscillate between the viewpoints of Dr. Y, the objective observer, and Ted, the attuned participant. Dr. Y needs to mess around in the "in-between" and those who are already there must be aware that it might not always be best to wait for the discovery of a personal insight to intervene. I am not suggesting that Ted actually waited until he drove an old car to work to make an intervention reconnecting Mr. D to his painful memories about his old car; nonetheless, it was a lucky guess based on a mistaken assumption that the analysand had not seen his car. Successful as it was in this instance, many interventions based on the analyst's associations might not resonate or might even fail to connect. I wondered as I read whether the analyst who believes he is attuned is aware of how many times such interventions will be experienced as suggestions and create compliance to the analyst's empathic brilliance. At the least, the attuned analyst must be aware both of the transference implications of being so attuned that he prevents the analysand from using the method to discover for herself what the analyst's empathy provides, and the countertransference possibility that the analyst doesn't want to be shown that he is out of tune.

Dr. Y, in contrast, would not face this difficulty, privileging as he does the cooperation of the analysand with the analytic method. Ever alert to this, he might have rejected the intervention on the grounds that it gratified Mr. D's silently expressed transference demand for the analyst to speak first. He, then, might have made a resistance interpretation of the meaning of silence and tried to obtain Mr. D's associations which would certainly have been to his experience with his father. Or, he might have said nothing and thereby refused a transference demand for him to speak and interpreted this later; or, he might have commented on the "rotating movement of his hands" in such a way as to enable Mr. P to transform an action into words. These interventions might have led to the same goal as Ted's. If the analyst's personal history does not contain experiences that provide a pathway to make the right guess for the wrong reason, Dr. Y's ideas provide many ways to solve the problem of an initial silence. I think analysts who are less attracted to finding attuned ways to intervene pay more attention to other analytic techniques that derive from the objective observer tradition, and those that wish to make empathic interventions may miss opportunities to improve their analysands' ability to use the analytic method. I thought that each technique has its advantages and disadvantages. Empathic comments can lead to transference gratifications that need to be interpreted instead of enacted; insisting on the method can be at the expense of enabling the analysand to feel understood.

In short, I am suggesting that there are two trends in the relationship between the analyst and the analysand that need to be balanced and not separated into the disagreement between Dr. Y and Ted. They both should be able to be objective observers and attuned listeners (see Spencer and Balter, 1990, in this regard). From other contacts with Ted I have no doubt that he combines both in his work even though I suspect he might, on occasion, be reluctant to use techniques that Dr. Y uses exclusively because they might not feel empathic. I am more concerned that Dr. Y does not use the attunement ideas Ted advances because he does not admit that Ted's ideas are useful. If that is true, his analysands cannot benefit from the advances made since the days when the science of psychoanalysis was defined in terms of the philosophy of Positivism. I trust that Ted will not allow the matter to rest with Dr. Y as a simple disagreement with two equally satisfactory points of view. I suggest that Ted and Dr. Y could agree that each should use a balanced proportion of each other's approach to psychoanalysis by being more sympathetic to the good in each.

THE RELATIONSHIP BETWEEN READING AND THE ANALYTIC PROCESS

In my discussion so far, I selected a few of the comments I made in response to the text and elaborated on them to have a mental conversation with Ted. For example, I followed his discussion with Dr. Y and was able to respond empathically to Ted's disagreement with him. Dr. Y seemed to believe in his ability to read the text of an analysand's productions without interference from his own unconscious, and Ted sought to persuade him that this is not always reliable. To prove his point Ted illustrated how Dr. Y's unresolved mourning for his father blocked his ability to understand that the analysand feared losing Dr. Y and defended himself against this attachment. Dr. Y used his dream to discover the connection between his own feelings of loss for his father and the analysand's concern about losing him. Ted's idea that no one is so completely analyzed that such personal countertransference blind spot will not occur is in agreement with my own views, and I became concerned that Dr. Y was an old fashioned "Positivist," or a Mr. Spock.

Because I followed the rest of my reading of Ted's paper by indicating my immediate responses jotted in the margin, I showed how a reader's dialogue with a text begins. It is strikingly similar to how the dialogue with an analysand begins. Immediate empathic connections with the author or the analysand occur and may be in need of revision as the empathic identification breaks down in the light of further evidence. This is what has happened in regard to my view of Dr. Y. Initially my empathic connection with Ted based on my prior relationship with him silently transformed into a shared belief with his view that Dr. Y exemplified an antiquated view of psychoanalysis. The paradox I noted in my spontaneous marginal notes—that Dr. Y was highly esteemed by Ted for his clinical brilliance while practicing an old-fashioned understanding of psychoanalysis—receded into the background, and I ignored the contradictory information. My transference to Ted's viewpoint accounts for my initial unbalanced comments about Dr. Y that culminated in my saying that he did not understand the significance of his own dream that enabled Dr. Y to understand his analysand. Was this a fair conclusion? I think not. I was taking Ted's position toward Dr. Y' s inability to elevate countertransference to the same level of importance as Ted did and was not satisfied with Dr. Y's claim that his unconscious was on Ted's side. In retrospect I now believe they did use his dream to take into account his own unconscious blind spots, and that he remained serious in his inability to endorse Ted's way of working.

My transference to Ted's idea reached its highest point when I considered the answers to the four questions posed by Ted, and used this to criticize Dr. Y. This can be construed to be a form of literary "acting out" in which I trashed Dr. Y for Ted. This bears a close similarity to certain forms of analysands "acting out" what they believe their analyst desires but does not do. It often happens in the beginning of analysis, and the cautious analyst learns to be aware of the tendency to take sides too soon. If a discussant does not take into account the similarity between reading and treating the potential for acting out a positive or negative transference can easily occur. Because I deliberately allowed myself the luxury of forming an empathic attunement to Ted this process unfolded in the text of my discussion.

The dissolution of my transference to the Ted's viewpoint began when I described Ted's discussion of Reiser's (1997) work as a detour into neurology. I reasoned that if his psychological explanations were sufficient, it was not necessary to buttress them by the biological substrate in which they occur. Further questioning of Ted's ideas—a falling out of attunement—occurs when I question his use of the term "analyzing instrument" (Isakower, 1963) and suggest the idea of tuning two violins. Unfortunately, when I originally gave this discussion, I had limited time and could not fully discuss Ted's work with his two analysands. I will now rectify this shortcoming.

THE CLINICAL SITUATION

In the case of Mr. D. Ted observes that an interview begins with an unusual period of silence and an appearance of sadness on the part of his analysand. He then notes that Mr. D's hands move as if he is driving a car. Feeling perplexed Ted allows his mind to drift during the silence and remembers that his analysand experienced a painful episode during his adolescence that involved his father disappointing him. Ted then recalled that he drove to work in an old car and did not believe Mr. D saw him arrive. His personal associations were to an old car he was ashamed to drive when he was eighteen. The similarity of their experiences enabled Ted to come into empathic attunement with Mr. D and explore more thoroughly his disappointment in Ted's loss of status when Mr. D saw him driving an old car. But, Ted did not think that Mr. D saw him and therefore had no reason to know what his hand movements represent. I described the empathic connection as a lucky guess on Ted's part. What I imply by this is that Ted had many other options to use to discover the meaning of Mr. D's puzzling hand movements. He would have used them had he not had a similar experience with a car, a fact that can be considered a coincidence not available to any other analyst working with Mr. D. Instead of a lucky guess as to the meaning of the driving hand motions, Ted could have discovered it through use of the analytic method that would have served as well because it enables body language to be translated into verbal associations. My guess is that this approach is precisely what Dr. Y would have used validating his claim that empathic attunement based on a similarity of life experiences is not as necessary as Ted implies. The issue here is not, as Ted claims, to decide whether to disclose or not disclose personal information to the analysand. Rather, the issue is to decide whether or not the analytic method can be used to resolve such puzzling actions.

In the second example, a typical countertransference blind spot is described in which Ted does not realize that his relationship with his withdrawn grandfather whom he longed to know prevented him from responding to Mr. K who behaved in a similar way. He resolved the problem with his analysand by becoming so frustrated that he became angry with Mr. K. In doing so he stepped out of an analytic stance and demonstrated he was not just an emotionally neutral observer of him from the "withdrawn" position of the analytic stance. Again the issue of interest is not that such emotionally charged events happen because no analyst is perfectly analyzed so that he has no blind spots. The issue is can the analytic method be improved sufficiently so that the need to enact the countertransference feelings is lessened. Dr. Y believes that he depends less on the similarity between the analyst's life experiences and the analysand's life experiences as a means to resolve impasses in analysis. Ted believes that the analytic method will not suffice and that the use of empathic attunement based on one's own personal history can enable the analyst to resolve problems which the method cannot address.

A LAST BIT OF SELF-REFLECTION

Let me return to the last paragraph of the section of my discussion that is titled "Attunement and Objectivity." Upon further reflection, I would revise it in the light of the resolution of my positive transference to Ted and my negative transference to Dr. Y. I would no longer be more concerned about Dr. Y's work with his analysands than I would be with Ted's work. Instead, I would be comfortable with the idea that both trust in the analytic method so highly valued by Dr. Y and the belief of Ted that empathic attunement are essential aspects of the analyst's skills. A balanced view of the assets and liabilities of each serve the best interests of the analysand. Further, I suggest that the reader of an analytic paper must attend to the transference and countertranference potentials elicited by the author so that he can develop a balanced appreciation of the author's contributions.

REFERENCES

Bion, W. R. 1967. Notes on memory and desire. *Psychoanalytic Forum* 2: 271–280.

Isakower, O. 1963a. Minutes of the New York Psychoanalytic Institute faculty meeting, October 14, unpublished.

———.1963b. Minutes of the New York Psychoanalytic Institute faculty meeting, November 20, unpublished.

Reich, A. 1951. On countertransference. *International Journal of Psychoanalysis* 41: 389–395.

Spencer, J. H. and L. Balter. 1990. Psychoanalytic observation. *Journal of the American Psychoanalytic Association* 38: 393–421.

8

Relatedness and Listening

A Concluding Commentary

M. Hossein Etezady, M.D.

Separation-individuation process as formulated by Mahler and her coworkers (1975) can be viewed as an aspect of psychological development that leads to learning how to be alone in the presence of an 'Other.' Implicit relational knowing which begins early in infancy and evolves through subsequent developmental stages and age-related events guides the dynamic course of one's relationship with others and determines the quality and character of essential relationships in one's life. As separation-individuation process, by thirty-six months of age culminates in the establishment of a beginning on the way to object constancy, the four-year-old child's sense of self is more stable, objective, and capable of maintaining relative cohesion in the face of the growing demands of reality aided by the emergence of secondary process thinking, secondary narcissism, and the depressive position.

Mahler's theory of separation individuation grew out of observations of interaction between children and their mothers and was based on the ego psychological, structural and object-relations lexicon of its time. Mahler's symposia, originated by the late Selma Kramer in Philadelphia, have repeatedly brought together divergent perspectives in clinical and research application, establishing bridges with attachment theory and research, self-psychology, cognitive psychology, and intersubjectivity. What we have learned since Mahler's original research has augmented, clarified, and expanded our understanding of separation-individuation as a developmental process and have added to our knowledge about pre-oedipal development and related pathological formations. Separation-individuation theory views the intra-psychic experience from an interpersonal perspective and can look at interpersonal elements from an intra-psychic point of view. It can therefore uniquely accommodate to one person or two person psychology, conflict theory and transition from a dyadic, pre-oedipal intersubjective mode of relatedness to an oedipal, triadic, narrative mode of relatedness in the depressive position. It can illuminate the dynamics of self and interactive regulation and the influence of 'the first relationship' on the future course of object-relations and the enduring quality of one's attachment. Separation-individuation theory provides a conceptual frame that can accommodate to diverse perspectives on pre-oedipal development and the subsequent events of the life cycle. It is capable of integrating new and complementary findings from the clinical setting or in the context of research and evidence-based data collection.

In what follows I hope to show how major contributions of divergent conceptual perspectives in today's marketplace of expanding knowledge and diversity of methods and techniques can be pulled together as compatible and complementary aspects of a single enterprise we know as psychoanalysis, rather than taking apart each new impression critically and with an eye to discrediting or discarding whatever doesn't seem to belong to one or another of our favorite conceptual frames.

SCHWABER'S CONTRIBUTION

Evelyne Schwaber recalls the impact of her exposure to Mahler's teachings and pioneering work of infant observation. She pays tribute to Mahler for her contribution to psychoanalytic theory and infant observation, thereby revolutionizing our way of looking at mother-child relationships and communication. I wish to join Schwaber in paying tribute to the work of Mahler, Pine, and Bergman (1975). In their work they formulated separation-individuation process as a developmental sequence by which we can map the path to the eventual establishment of the beginning of self and object constancy by the end of the pre-oedipal period. Self and object constancy are considered to be the end result of the normal course of separation-individuation and are required for age-appropriate self and interactive regulation of the oedipal and subsequent periods of development. Without the establishment of the beginnings of self and object constancy, affect modulation, affect integration and affect containment are impeded. Signal affects do not emerge and primitive defenses of splitting and projection will continue to dominate. Impulse control, frustration tolerance, and self-cohesion are lacking. Narcissistic equilibrium is sought through coercive omnipotent control of the object in an anal-sadistic mode or by schizoid withdrawal into an internal void of unconscious fantasy.

Bergman and Harpaz-Rotem (2004) consider Stern's (1985) view of the emergence of intersubjectivity close to the end of the first year, following differentiation, as more consequential than upright locomotion, which Mahler viewed as the most significant event at this time. It is at this time that the child begins to learn how to be alone in the presence of an other. With the advent of rapprochement in the latter half of the second year, (from about fifteen to twenty-four months), the child and the mother are both faced with the challenging task of learning a *new* way of being together. The child's attempt to re-create the blissfully powerful sense of dual unity once the fuel for his love affair with the world now leads to his disillusionment, bewilderment, and rage. Mother's ability to maintain libidinal availability during this time and to contain, neutralize and survive the rage sets a pattern of disruption and recovery in the wake of despondency and loss of control. Maternal attunement and empathic resonance is essential in intuitively "getting" the message and providing the consistency and predictability that the toddler needs if he is able to integrate the dichotomous experience of integrating the mental representations of the beloved symbiotic object with the hated source of separation, frustration and opposition, in a unitary consistency of a secure attachment, capable of allowing and amplifying assertiveness and self-agency. In the absence of achievement of the beginnings of self and object constancy, realistic assessment of the self and others is not possible and the capability to make beneficial use of available self-objects is impaired. Implicit relational knowing is faulty. Self-reflective function, mentalization, and empathy are not available and seeing oneself from the perspective of an other is not possible. These individuals are not capable of 'locating' oneself within an other.

Many of our patients' problems have their roots in these early experiences and in arrested development in this pre-oedipal mode. In analytic intervention with this group empathic resonance, and unambiguous responsiveness through locating oneself within an other is mandatory. In these individuals we are not uncovering or reconstructing elements of past events or discrete memories, as we are instead providing opportunities for the patient to participate in a supportive and consistent relationship capable of holding, containing, sustaining, and reflecting empathically the subjective state of the patient. It is in the emotional milieu of such a therapeutic relationship that self-cohesion can be experienced, established, reached for, and in time duplicated. Pathological constellation in these instances can be varied and often very severe. Analytically informed intervention with these individuals requires reworking of the anal-sadistic modes or relatedness and the unresolved issues or rapprochement in the context of transference whereby the therapist provides developmental assistance in the role of a 'real object' and not merely offering abstract reconfiguration or only 'interpretation,' as a transference object.

With mother's auxiliary ego providing self-object functions of a reliable and restorative nature, the child learns to bounce back from frustration, defeat, and disillusionment and recover through the use of his own self-righting capacities. From twenty-four to thirty-six months and following the resolution of rapprochement, there is a period of consolidation that results in completing the task of establishing the beginnings of self and object constancy and completes the transition from primary to secondary narcissism, from primary process thinking to secondary process thinking and from splitting to fusion. Mothers whose empathic attunement is deficient for any of a large variety of reasons, will be more likely to respond with measures that do not meet their child's self-object needs and thereby contribute to the emergence of the 'terrible twos' which can remain unresolved into later life. In these circumstances, primary narcissism and primary process thinking continue to dominate and anal-sadistic mode of relatedness will persist. When rapprochement has not been resolved and the drives have not been fused, self and object relations are split and emotional stability cannot be maintained. Self and interactive regulation fails to sustain cohesion in the face of frustration. Our metapsychology also informs us that since aggression has not been sufficiently neutralized, ego growth, ego resources, and superego are under developed and primitive. Impulse delay and control, affect modulation, repression, sublimation, and higher defenses are not effectively available.

'Getting it' connotes the epitome of managing to grasp something, as if in a physical grip, at the center of one's awareness. To 'get it' means to experience the hard-core reality of a message. Getting it goes beyond words and surpasses boundaries of intuition and logic. If one is sympathetic and therefore compassionately open, empathic resonance is more likely and more liable to be gratifying. Empathic resonance or openness to such resonance is not as likely when one is depleted, emotionally unavailable or adverse to exposure to negative affect.

Adverse exposure during unwelcome emergence of negative affective content sets in motion defensive patterns, and character traits that are rooted in development, one's history, unconscious motivation and implicit or procedural memory. In therapeutic encounters we tolerate such exposure in the service of our professional objective, ethics, and values. Indeed, it is our capacity to tolerate and contain the affect which allows the patient to engage in therapeutic alliance and working through of the transference.

Schwaber tells of a patient's concern that complaining about her depression would hurt the doctor who represents the mother in the transference. There are many times when as members of the healing profession we are engaged in the care of extreme circumstances that may involve severe pain, death, lust, disruption, trauma, illness, catastrophe, and personal or family tragedies. Consciously we choose the challenge and responsibility of helping, in our part of the process. We need to be vigilant about the effects of factors outside of our consciousness that influence our choices and determine the form and character of our predilections and personal styles. We know how certain individuals or particular issues affect us and we try to find our own workspace with such disturbing encounters. Like the proverbial surgeon, we see ourselves getting in, doing no harm, finishing the job, and closing, unaffected and intact, to the eventual benefit of the patient whose well-being depends on this often heroic intervention.

The objectivity, precision, and neutrality of such a posture for us may be intriguing, and ideally straightforward. But ideal surgeons in their decisive and objective stance are not, and cannot, always be neutral or unaffected. In our work, we are the main instrument. Our method is the personal experience of penetrating immersion in the subjective universe of our patient. The therapeutic instrument or the 'analytic third' (Ogden, 1994) includes our totality as one main agent in the intersubjective co-creation that contains the therapeutic process.

Another conceptual model for a therapeutic relationship may be structured from a developmental perspective in the context of 'the first relationship.' In the maternal aspect of our analytic encounter our function is to hold, contain, reflect, and empathically resonate while representing reality. The holding and containing, reflecting and mentalizing aspect of the treatment process may not be as crucially indispensable in all cases. For example, many high functioning, healthier individuals contending mainly with neurotic conflicts of a triadic nature, need and are better able to make constructive use of our neutral objectivity since they can contain and regulate their own upheavals and maintain cohesion in the face of regression, optimal frustration or unresolved conflicts. The majority of our patients, however, do not possess sufficient degrees of this capability, as they may be too young, developmentally arrested, or otherwise incapable of adequate self-regulation. There are individuals who require "developmental assistance" in analytically informed intervention. We provide transference gratification or respond in the form of enactment when such developmental assistance is unnecessary or contraindicated. We may be taking refuge to a pre-oedipal stance, for example, in defending against the patient's unconscious erotic or aggressive material of an oedipal nature. Such misreading of our analytic encounter based on unresolved countertransference reactions poses the risk of stalemate, negative therapeutic reaction, interminable or disrupted treatment, and boundary violation. We are vigilant to signs of countertransference expression in our self analysis and in understanding the influence of the patient's unconscious on ours.

Schwaber takes us beyond the obvious and the routinely expressed, to the minutely deciphered nuances of humanity that enrich and enliven a relationship; the art and for those who have it, the gift of listening from the perspective of an other; a truly object centered view. 'Getting it ' as Schwaber defines, is nevertheless difficult as she amply exposes and it takes self-reflection and the kind of healthy narcissism that can tolerate being moved internally, from one to another, new position, after having emerged from locating oneself within an other.

JACOBS'S CONTRIBUTION

Theodore Jacobs's contribution is rich, persuasive, and enlightening not only for its illuminating content and the voice of long experience in which it is stated, but for the important questions it raises and the variety of answers that it invites us to entertain.

From the beginning of my career I came to the conclusion based on my work with my patients and exposure to the literature and the work of others, that one could assume an order of priority as to what elements in the analyst's armamentarium matter most. I used the acronym ESTO to stand for Empathy, Style, Technique, and Orientation. This was to stress the notion that theoretical orientation, technical expertise, conscious and unconscious aspects of the analyst's personal style in communication and application of interactive nuance, matter greatly and influence the treatment process in numerous respects. However, without empathy all other elements can fall to the wayside no matter how highly polished the style, soundly maintained the technique or well-grounded the orientation.

When empathic attunement is present and navigates the course of intervention, all other elements begin to combine and are capable of functioning as a dynamic unity and can respond in confirmatory holding, palliative containment, and neutralizing reflection, sometimes in the form of interpretations that bring together elements of the understanding from the deep and the past to the now and the surface, and from subjective to objective, and from ambiguity and mystery to clarity and mastery.

Even in the course of supportive and infrequent therapeutic contact, the most important element for achieving the goals of treatment is empathy. Empathy at its developmentally basic level requires the capacity to see the world and an experience from more than one solitary personal perspective. The capacity to imagine an experience from the perspective of an other is the heir to the development of self and object constancy which becomes functionally available by the beginning of the fourth year. From here on it is subject to the vicissitudes of the oedipal resolution and subsequent life events. Empathic capacity can grow with experience, with conscious effort at attunement and through deeper self-understanding. It is unavailable in the absence of self and object constancy and it can be impaired in narcissistic withdrawal or narcissistic pathology. It is more readily on track in the context of familiarity. Those we do not know or do not understand as well as those we fear or doubt are less likely to stimulate our empathic receptivity. There are unconscious as well as conscious mechanisms of attunement which in therapeutic interaction we need to keep within usable access.

I mention my longstanding devotion to the centrality of empathy at this point because after all "listening" is the main ingredient of our intervention and presumably constitutes the lion's share of our therapeutic activity. Not merely listening passively and in isolation, but actively listening, well-attuned, in full presence and with all of our perceptual and intuitive resources, with evenly hovering attention. Not just to the words but to the essence they intend to convey, the affective quality, quantity, and means of expression. Listening for the impact of the subjective sense of the experience the patient conveys, verbalized either in a free associative narrative or in reactive exigency.

Words are not the best containers or conveyors of emotions and subjective states. Emotional expressions search for words but are experienced in somatic, physical, and organic terms. They are readily manifested nonverbally in body language or behavior. So in listening to our patients we hear words that represent the reality of their experience only to a limited extent. By trying to integrate the verbal and nonverbal expression together with the body language and by setting our analytic instrument receptively to the totality of the patient's experience, we try to gain an empathic grasp of parts of the patient's subjective universe. Empathic attunement is the heart and the soul, of evocative listening as Jacobs asserts. 'Evocative listening' allows us to form impressions and intuitive perceptions that bring together the patient's communicated message and its overt and covert content together with our own conscious and unconscious reactions. Evocative listening in this way is capable of forming a coherent approximation of what our patient's subjective experience is likely to be.

We set out to engage our conscious faculties with those of the patient, but major unconscious contributions from both sides of the therapeutic divide operate powerfully in the mix and together create what may be described as an intersubjective experiential co-construct. As the experiential essence of a relationship the intersubjective immersion contains elements that are unique and specific to each individual interaction. It is what makes relationships intuitive, familiar, predictable, unique, and sustainable.

In evocative listening, a la Jacobs, we set our conscious mind, focused on our patient's expressions, verbal or otherwise and allow our intuition, fantasies, reveries, and dreams to tell us where the impact of the patient's unconscious on ours may be taking us. Evocative listening delivers impressions and pictures that can be tested and explored against the flow of the patient's material and the past experiential context that adds meaning to the experience of the present moment.

Jacobs tells us we need empathy but empathy alone is not sufficient for reaching the attunement of the analytic instrument at its best.

Jacobs's contemplative quandaries viewed in the order of priorities suggested by my acronym ESTO places style in the second most important position in this hierarchy. The style of our communication, intervention, our own personal way of being alone in the presence of an other, and the distinguishing features in our habitual mode of conduct is rooted in the basic and intimately enduring foundations of our self-organization. It arises from the center of the self and carries with it our developmental and object relations history. Our style emanates from our personality. All styles are not equally well suited to all situations or to every patient. Some styles and orientations may be problematic in particular circumstances or may be especially facilitating in others.

Technique is placed next in this order. Skillful application of principles and methods we have learned through training and have honed through practice and experience is the ultimate objective of a clinician. Technique as a therapeutic skill is what we value and hope to fine tune over time. It is the consummation of our clinical dexterity and prowess, flexibly and effectively applied in the right time and circumstance. Essentials or minutiae of technique may need to change from one to another situation or one individual to another. Given empathy and a suitable fit in style and compatibility, technical facility can go a long way in furthering treatment process.

Orientation in theory and school of thought as the last in this order can subsume application of technique and the individual's personal style of delivery and interaction. I place orientation at the bottom of this list and consider it nearly immaterial in the absence of empathic attunement. Intervention based on empathy has a chance of hitting the mark, but without it there may be no mark to aim for, regardless of one's theoretical orientation, technical expertise, or personal style. When we "get it" and resonate with the patient's subjective experience, we are likely to be helpful and effective regardless of the specifics of style, technique, or orientation.

BENJAMIN'S CONTRIBUTION

Jessica Benjamin makes a highly nuanced and detailed exposition of a viewpoint which is eloquently summarized in her statement that she tries to teach her patient how to help in keeping open the possibility of mutual containment at all times. While this mutuality is an eventual objective to work toward, initially it may be no more realistic to expect it in the treatment setting than it would be in the context of the relationship of a mother to her baby. Self-containment initially, and later the capacity to hold in mind the state of the mind of an other, by age four, are developmentally possible only in the context of having been held and contained as the emerging self-organization becomes the core self and then differentiates to enter the intersubjective state of self-experience. Here is where the child first learns to be alone in the presence of an other (Winnicott, 1963). During the practicing subphase of separation-individuation and well into the first quarter of the second year, the infant toddler's buoyancy and drive to seek and master novelty, learning and exploring is regenerated and energized through refueling and darting, in an exuberant relationship with the mother. With the increase in the awareness of the sense of separateness and the episodes of failure and disruption in the 'symbiotic' magical quality of the experience in the relationship with the mother, the child and the mother are both challenged with the complicated task of having to learn a new way of being together. Rapprochement, spanning over the last several months of the second year, and a period of further consolidation spanning from about twenty-four to thirty-six months create and establish this new way of relatedness. When this process moves on optimally by thirty-six months of age, the average child in the beginning of his fourth year and on the threshold of the oedipal period has begun to lay down early foundations of self and object constancy. Attainment of self and object constancy is an accomplishment of a relative nature which continues to evolve and stabilize throughout the life cycle. Object constancy determines the quality of self-experience, self-regulation, interactive regulation, and the nature of the future essential relationships.

Again, I am highlighting the importance of object constancy, the heir to resolution of rapprochement, because such failure in the pre-oedipal period requires different therapeutic elements and technique as compared to oedipal pathology. When such pre-oedipal pathology is the dominant presentation of the clinical picture, enduring structural intra-psychic change and transformation will require a reliving and reworking of unresolved rapprochement issues which in time will lead to integration, fusion, and establishing of the beginnings of object constancy. This will then allow for gradual reorganization and transition from the dyadic, sadomasochistic, or paranoid-schizoid mode of relatedness to a triadic-narrative and oedipal mode. In this mode the idealization/devaluation splitting of primary narcissism has evolved into secondary narcissism as manifested in the capability to experience the self as related to but separate from the object who is recognized and appreciated for its own independent needs and attributes and as a separate locus of agency and responsibility. Mentalization (Fonagy and Target, 1997) empathy, self reflection, and the depressive position, all grounded in presence of the early beginnings of self and object constancy, allow for containment of affects and tolerance of ambivalence, loss, and pain, in the service of self-regulation as well as mutual and interactive regulation.

What I find most illuminating and clinically pertinent in Benjamin's presentation is her clear description of the analytic process as she juxtaposes split aspects of the self and object representations on the one hand and the role of the analyst as a real object in the context of transference on the other. When we fail to tolerate, recognize, and contain the negative and potentially destructive aggressive components of the transference, we may be unconsciously colluding in protecting dissociated self-experiences that may be pressing toward the surface. This collusion eliminates the possibility of any healing of the split since recognizing, tolerating, accepting, and accommodating to the negative experience, first by the analyst and in time by the patient, will not be possible.

Benjamin skillfully and sensitively enumerates various paths in the process of disruption and repair as a healing element as well as those that lead us into dissociation, complementarity, collusion, and failure. In fact we are led to believe that it is the "moral third" in the therapeutic instrument of 'thirdness' (Ogden, 1994) that allows us to learn from our mistakes and failures, if we are able to regulate our own narcissistic need to disavow failure or vulnerability, so that we may be able to anticipate, experience, and acknowledge the failure or the disruption and to resonate with the dissociated aspects of the patient's experience that may be pressing for recognition behind a wall of disavowal, splitting and dissociation.

Reflecting upon the adversarial question that might be posed as to how one plus one amounts to two plus a third, as implied in the notion of the analytic third, I offer the following thought. When it is one subject plus an other, the total would of course still be two, yet in addition we have created an intersubjective entity that is neither one or the other, but a co-construction consisting of parts of each individual subject focused on the therapeutic process. This new entity is co-created in and is entirely unique to the intersubjective field of this particular dyadic relationship. Viewed in this light the analytic third can be expected to exist and may be attended, examined, enhanced, disrupted, or repaired. In this pursuit, Benjamin discusses elements not only involved in enactment induced by countertransference pitfalls but she also introduces the intriguing notion of *in-actment* which does no less harm than when countertransference blindspots prevent us from acting to repair the analytic third when needed and to abide by the objective directions of the moral third.

CONCLUDING REMARKS

'Getting it' by locating oneself within an other, a la Schwaber, empathic attunement and evocative listening through the use of the analytic instrument a la Jacobs and recognition, acceptance, and efforts at repairing failure and disruption in mutuality and containment, as in Benjamin's evocation of an analytic third, together with my own view of primacy of empathic attunement as a factor outweighing style, technique, and orientation, converge around pre-oedipal and early developmental vicissitudes. These include differentiation, self organization, and intersubjectivity, before rapprochement and consolidation during the second and third years of life can culminate in establishment of object constancy ushering in the narrative, triadic, oedipal mode of relatedness. The average child on the threshold of the fourth year, in an average expectable environment, traverses this successful passage on the way to object constancy, capable of empathy, mentalization, secondary process thinking and secondary narcissism. Mahler's (1975) theory of separation-individuation process sheds light on endless intricacy of these crucial human capabilities.

Psychoanalysis in clinical practice as well as in observational research is more intimately concerned and knowledgeable about relationships than any other field of intervention. From the mother child relationship and its developmental phases to interacting with others later in life or in the course of treatment, both as a 'real object' or a 'transference object' we use the relationship as a context for the experience and as an instrument for healing, growth, change, and transformation. In psychoanalytic treatment we emphasize essentials of the subjective experience and the capacity to see the world and grasp an experience from the perspective of another individual's subjective experience. This calls upon the capacity for self-reflection, objective judgment, and mentalization. These capacities each can only exist and develop in the context of 'the first relationship' initially and those subsequent relationships that matter to us most later on. The relationship as a self-object function and as a context for experience is founded on self and interactive regulation. This is possible when the separation-individuation process, via resolution of rapprochement, has allowed the child, by the beginning of the fourth year, to have started 'on the way to object constancy.' The organizational as well as the subjective aspects of self-experience vary in time, context, and manifestation. We are all aware of different states of self-experience even in the course of the same day. Our current-self, teacher-self, moral-self, playful-self, creative-self, warring-self, or vulnerable-self are needed and may surface at different degrees at different times. But we mostly operate as a wholesome, cohesive, and integrated self that can mold, adapt, and accommodate. Not only do we experience different self states, we live through varying and diverse modes and states of relatedness.

Relatedness as a state emerges out of the undifferentiated matrix of self-object experiences of the emerging self and the core self of the first weeks and months. Relatedness as a subjective experience can be appreciated once differentiation has begun and the self/other boundaries are beginning to be established. Relatedness at this juncture is a product of intersubjectivity and comprises the real essence of being alone in the presence of an other. As an element of the intersubjective experience, relatedness as a state can vary in qualitative or quantitative dimensions and involves procedural, unconscious, and conscious elements. A state of relatedness can be seen as a dynamic and context sensitive by-product of the interconnection between the two poles of a dyadic partnership. The mode of relatedness in the first weeks and months of the first year can be defined as monadic in nature. During the latter part of the first year and with the emergence of intersubjectivity, the mode of relationship becomes dyadic. The triadic mode of relatedness can exist after the late pre-oedipal events of the second and third years have resulted in establishing a beginning on the way to object constancy.

While the three modes of relatedness, that is monadic, dyadic, and triadic, enter the scene in sequential order in early childhood, subsequently they can be present singly or in combination at all times. Being alone in the presence of an 'other' (whether family, friends, therapist or one's object of faith) is facilitated, learned, and fine-tuned as implicit relational knowing primarily in the context of "the first relationship" and later in the expanding circles of connections that grow out of attachment patterns of the first relationship.

In the three main contributions to this book, we encounter the voices of three experts. Schwaber specifies a state of relatedness within the analytic process which locates one within an other in order to make "getting it" possible. This means knowing and understanding the patient's experience from his personal perspective rather than our own. Jacobs describes a state of relatedness in which there is a two-way stream of unconscious and reciprocal influence. Empathic attunement within this state of mutuality allows for creative use of the analyst's intuitive, subjective, personal and primary process impingements and can place countertransference in the service of empathy and evocative listening rather than a compelling source of enactment, impeding the analytic process.

Benjamin describes the analytic process in terms of a state of relatedness that fosters mutual containment and attending to an analytic third that can be creatively generated, maintained, repaired, and revitalized throughout the 'messy' and vacillating course of disruption, which is inevitable and restorative repair, which is desirable in all mutual states of relatedness and in the analytic process in particular.

REFERENCES

Bergman, A., and I. Harpaz-Rotem, I. 2004. Revisiting rapprochement in the light of contemporary developmental theories. *Journal of the American Psychoanalytic Association* 52: 555–570.

Fonagy, P. and M. Target. 1997. Attachment and reflective function: their role in self-organization. *Development and Psychopathology* 9: 679–700.

Mahler, M. S., F. Pine, and A. Bergman. 1975. *The Psychological Birth of the Human Infant.* New York: Basic Books.

Ogden, T. 1994. *Subject of Analysis.* Northvale, NJ: Jason Aronson.

Stern, D. 1985. *The Interpersonal World of the Infant.* New York: Basic Books.

Winnicott, D. W. 1963. The development of the capacity for concern. In: *The Maturational Processes and the Facilitating Environment*, pp. 73–82. New York: International Universities Press, 1965.

About the Editor and Contributors

Salman Akhtar, M.D., is professor of psychiatry at Jefferson Medical College and training and supervising analyst at the Psychoanalytic Center of Philadelphia. His scientific publications include twenty-nine authored and edited books. In addition, he has published six volumes of poetry.

Jessica Benjamin, Ph.D., faculty member and supervisor at the post-doctoral psychology program in psychoanalysis and psychotherapy, New York University, co-founder of the International Association for Relational Psychoanalysis and Psychotherapy, Private Practice.

M. Hossein Etezady, M.D., clinical director of psychiatric services, Paoli Memorial Hospital, and faculty member, Psychoanalytic Center of Philadelphia.

Theodore Fallon, M.D., faculty member, Psychoanalytic Center of Philadelphia.

Theodore J. Jacobs, M.D., clinical professor of psychiatry, Albert Einstein College of Medicine, New York University School of Medicine, supervising and training analyst, New York and New York University

Psychoanalytic Institutes, supervising child analyst, New York University Psychoanalytic Institute.

Sydney E. Pulver, M.D., supervising and training analyst, Psychoanalytic Center of Philadelphia.

David M. Sachs, M.D., supervising and training analyst, Psychoanalytic Center of Philadelphia.

Evelyne Albrecht Schwaber, M.D., supervising and training analyst, Psychoanalytic Institute of New England East, faculty member, Boston Psychoanalytic Society and Institute.

www.ingramcontent.com/pod-product-compliance
Ingram Content Group UK Ltd.
Pitfield, Milton Keynes, MK11 3LW, UK
UKHW012042150926
475560UK00001B/139

9 780765 705143